Praise for *Carving a Niche for Himself*

"Luigi Del Bianco may not be a household nan.. .. ....y historians, but he should be. He played an integral role in the creation of Mount Rushmore, specifically, that of chief carver. Was Del Bianco slighted due to his Italian heritage? Gladstone more than suggests he was. This book will be an inspiration to Italian Americans everywhere, and sheds new light on the role of Italians in America's history."

Marilyn Borner, Publisher
The Italian Tribune

"As a former major league ballplayer, I can tell you firsthand that nobody goes to bat for people who haven't gotten a fair shake in life better than Doug Gladstone."

Carmen Fanzone, Special Assistant to the President
Professional Musicians Local 47

"With an investigative reporter's ear for different voices and a researcher's enthusiasm for a variety of perspectives, Doug Gladstone's intriguing new book offers a multi-faceted, timely and vibrant account of Luigi Del Bianco and his role at Mount Rushmore. Gladstone's engaging work about the Italian-American immigrant who served as chief carver at the memorial is a gift to our national lore and to all immigrants, both past and present."

Camille Linen, Education Director
Port Chester Council on the Arts

"There have been many omissions in the telling of our Italian American story. However, thanks to Douglas J. Gladstone, the story of the contribution made by Lou Del Bianco's grandfather has not gone untold. Like so many immigrants, Luigi Del Bianco was proud to be an American, and showed his love and appreciation for his adopted country in his life's work. *Carving a Niche for Himself* reveals an important stone in America's multicultural foundation."

Dr. Joseph V. Scelsa
President & Chief Executive Officer
Italian American Museum of New York

VIA FOLIOS 95

Carving a Niche for Himself

The Untold Story of Luigi Del Bianco and Mount Rushmore

Douglas J. Gladstone

BORDIGHERA PRESS

Library of Congress Control Number: 2014931950

Printed in the United States.

Published by
BORDIGHERA PRESS
John D. Calandra Italian American Institute
25 West 43rd Street, 17th Floor
New York, NY 10036

VIA FOLIOS 95
ISBN 978-1-59954-067-2

TABLE OF CONTENTS

LIST OF PHOTOGRAPHS

Page xii • A nattily attired Luigi Del Bianco in Barre, Vermont circa 1910.

Page 6 • A partially completed Mount Rushmore, circa 1938, at a distance.

Page 26 • Luigi Del Bianco, sitting, in Barre, VT, circa 1913.

Page 62 • Luigi Del Bianco in Gutzon Borglum's studio at Mount Rushmore with the models for George Washington and Abraham Lincoln.

Page 63 • Luigi's three sons, circa 1935: from left are Silvio, Caesar and Lou's late father, Vincent Del Bianco.

Page 64 • Lou Del Bianco with the marble bust his late grandfather, Luigi, carved of himself in 1921.

Page 70 • Luigi Del Bianco and Primo Carnera.

Page 92 • Luigi Del Bianco with Native Americans.

Page 100 • Luigi Del Bianco with Lincoln Borglum.

Front Cover photo: Luigi working on Lincoln's eye, courtesy of Borglum Archives.

Back Cover photo: Lou Del Bianco performing his one-man show, "In the Shadow of the Mountain," during one of his special presentations in the sculptor's studio at Mount Rushmore on July 3, 2011. The actual presidential models that his grandfather worked on are in the background.

• • •

Unless otherwise noted, all photos are courtesy of the Del Bianco Family Collection.

ACKNOWLEDGMENTS

When I was 10-years-old, my late parents purchased me one of those old-fashioned View-Masters, the special stereoscope that allowed its user to look at 3-D pairs of small color photographs. One of the first set of reels I received was of the Mount Rushmore National Memorial.

When I looked at those faces through the View-Master, I was completely blown away by the sheer size of those carvings that had been made from the granite of the Black Hills mountains. I was particularly mesmerized by the eyes of the Four Presidents; they always looked like they were staring at me and only me.

Fast forward more than four decades, and I now know that Luigi Del Bianco was responsible for giving those four faces their refinement of expression.

But not too many other people know that.

Consequently, I set out to write a book that would help do for Luigi what my first book, *A Bitter Cup of Coffee*, did for nearly 900 retired Major League Ballplayers, namely, correct an egregious injustice.

Out of necessity, a journalist who writes a straight news story must always bring an unvarnished perspective to anything he or she writes. But as a proponent of advocacy journalism, I want to be up front with everyone who reads this book. Since I personally believe that Luigi has not been properly recognized for his contributions to the monument, I'm hoping that my work gets him the kudos that he is rightfully and richly deserving of.

Since I know my objectivity is going to be questioned, I invite you to make up your own mind and judge for yourself whether I have presented a fair and balanced account.

A nattily attired Luigi Del Bianco, in Barre, Vermont, circa 1910.

FOREWORD

It was during the early 1950s in the Bronx, New York, when I first learned about Mount Rushmore. My siblings and I would often rummage through the shoebox of family photos (they never made it to an album). We especially enjoyed the pictures of our mother and father during the time they lived in South Dakota in the early 1940s. At the time, my father was in the Army Air Force and stationed at Ellsworth Air Force Base near Rapid City.

Among the sepia-tinged photos of my parents and their friends in military garb were photos and postcards of Mount Rushmore during and after its creation. Even though I was only about 12 years old, I marveled at the scaffolding and ropes, and the workers they supported. The name Gutzon Borglum became lodged in my memory from reading the captions on the postcards. The man whose name I couldn't pronounce was responsible for this monumental sculpture. I was in awe.

My father often lamented his love of the Black Hills (my mother missed New York!). When we were kids, he spoke of it often and vowed to one day return. He never did. It was purely coincidental (I'm sure!) that in 1968, during my last six months serving in the Air Force, I received reassignment orders to Ellsworth Air Force Base. I recall reading my orders, scratching my head and not thinking at all, only feeling. I was going to see it. Rapid City, the Black Hills and Mount Rushmore.

Finally, in the Spring of 1968, with the old photos still fresh in my memory, I stood gazing at the mountain. I was moved. It was exactly what I knew it would be and once again Gutzon Borglum's name came to mind. But this time, I found myself wondering about the hundreds of other men and their roles in creating Mount

Rushmore. Unfortunately, I never made an effort to learn about any of them.

Recently, however, I learned that Mount Rushmore's Master Carver was Luigi Del Bianco, an Italian immigrant. Having been raised in an Italian household, where appreciation of the arts was taken very seriously, I remember thinking, "Well, no surprise here." My curiosity about Luigi soon became a quest to learn more about this overlooked sculptor. With the information I gathered, it was apparent that Luigi rose above adversity and took The American Dream to a whole new level. He epitomized achievement among Italian immigrants.

Luigi was one of thousands of Italian immigrants who came to America seeking a better life for himself and his family. Certainly not all were great artists or sculptors but most shared time-honored values and traditions typical of their generation: strong work ethic, pride in everything they did, and love of family. That's who they were.

Imagine Luigi's thoughts and feelings as he traversed the face of the mountain and sculpted the details of his *capolavoro* (masterpiece). Here was the man chosen to breathe life into the sculpture. Like Mount Rushmore, Luigi himself was a monumental figure. I suspect upon completion of his work, as artists typically do, he stepped back and silently burst with pride.

A well-deserved kudos to Gutzon Borglum, without whom Mount Rushmore would not exist. But in *Carving A Niche For Himself*, author Douglas J. Gladstone ushers Luigi to center stage. For without Luigi Del Bianco's exceptional talent and determination, Mount Rushmore would have no soul.

Robert Benedetto, Chairman
Benedetto Guitars, Inc.
Savannah, Georgia

Carving a Niche for Himself

INTRODUCTION

In *Bright Lights, Big City,* Jay McInerney's brilliant 1984 work that elevated the concept of second person narrative to new heights, his protagonist is a fact-checker for a major New York City publication. Being a recent graduate of Boston University, where I attained my Master's degree in Journalism, I was able to identify with his main character on some level. Mind you, I didn't relate to the drinking, drugs and partying he did, but I was able to appreciate his role at the magazine.

McInerney was able to grab me right from the start because he used a line from The Talking Head's song, "Crosseyed and Painless," to open his debut novel:

> Facts are simple and facts are straight,
> Facts are lazy and facts are late,
> Facts all come with points of view,
> Facts don't do what I want them to.[1]

In the narrative of the Mount Rushmore National Memorial — the one that the United States Department of the Interior's National Park Service puts out for public consumption — Gutzon and Lincoln Borglum are the only two individuals who are singled out for their work on what is one of the most renowned sculptures in the world.

The thing is, the Borglums didn't do the work alone. That is a fact.

As for anyone other than the Borglums, the policy of the Park

---

[1] "Crosseyed and Painless," from the album, *Remain in Light,* Talking Heads, 1980, Brian Eno, Producer.

very few people know that Luigi Del Bianco, who was born in Meduno, Italy, was the chief carver on what is arguably the most iconic of American landmarks.

If being the chief carver at Mount Rushmore is not the American dream for an immigrant to these lands, what is?

At some point or another in our lives, we have all felt the pain and sting of victimization, namely, we are not getting credit for things we worked on or conceived. Since that's a raw human emotion, which is very powerful, the story of Del Bianco clicked for me.

When it comes to the underdog, I'm a sucker for stories about people who have been wronged, unfairly treated or hosed. Since I'm of the Jewish faith, that's also part of my heritage.

Admittedly, I am not one of the most religious people in the world. However, what I like to believe I am is principled. Therefore, like a lot of Jews, I'm of the opinion that you can't have justice for yourself unless other people have justice as well.

It's my opinion that we should all have a little healthy respect for those who have been so slighted. For me, this tradition of helping others attain justice is best expressed in Zechariah 8:16 — the world stands on three things: on truth, on justice and on peace. Execute truth, justice and peace within your gates and, when truth is achieved, justice is done.

Also, in Pirkei Avot, that portion of the Talmud which teaches ethical principles, I once read that "the sword comes into the world because of justice delayed, because of justice perverted and because of those who render wrong decisions."

In my opinion, when it comes to Del Bianco, the Park Service has clearly made a wrong decision in its failure to tout his contributions at the monument. Fortunately, Luigi's grandson, Lou Del Bianco, is trying to do something about that.

I think it is important to, not only tell the story of Luigi Del Bianco, but tout the advocacy of Lou Del Bianco, as well. Lou has been vigilantly attempting to champion his late grandfather's contributions to Mount Rushmore ever since he discovered so many of the books that had been written about the memorial excluded Luigi.

I think he's right. And his efforts to remedy the situation are therefore commendable.

The reasons for Luigi Del Bianco's exclusion from so many of the books that have examined Rushmore are numerous and varied. As already mentioned, they include an age-old policy that administrators at the Park Service refuse to deviate from.

A second, and far more insidious and disturbing explanation, is offered up by Jim Sapione, a Del Bianco family friend who once served as the Supervisor of the Town of Rye, New York.

"It's very simple," says Sapione. "Luigi wasn't given the credit he was due because of a bias against Italian Americans, because of bigotry."

"We think it is a miscarriage of justice that the Park Service has failed to recognize Luigi Del Bianco's contribution," says Professor Philip J. DiNovo, chief executive officer of the national American Italian Heritage Association and Museum. "It is another sad example of Italian Americans not given the credit they have earned."

Ditto Dr. Manny Alfano, head of The Italian American ONE VOICE Coalition, the New Jersey-based organization whose mission, in part, is to secure the fair representation and equal treatment of Italian Americans.

"Luigi Del Bianco is a classic example of someone who did not receive equal recognition for his work, quite possibly because of an Italian last name and the fact that he was an immigrant," he said. "Few have heard his story, and we believe more should because it is indeed a great American success story."

Was Luigi Del Bianco as important as either of the Borglums, especially Gutzon, who he called his "master"? (Italians refer to their teachers as masters) Of course not. But, in keeping with the Park Service's own mission, how can the agency justify not telling Del Bianco's story?

The answer is, it can't. That's because facts don't do what we want them to.

A partially completed Mount Rushmore, circa 1938, at a distance.

CHAPTER 1

PORDENONE

B orn aboard a ship near La Havre, France on May 8, 1892, Luigi Del Bianco regularly hung around the wood carving shop that his father, Vincenzo, operated in the municipality of Meduno, which is in the northeast part of Italy. Both Vincenzo and his wife, Osvalda, were convinced that their son was not only interested in carving but, after seeing his first attempts to duplicate his father's work, had the ability to excel at it as well.

Meduno, which is located in the Province of Pordenone, is some 482 kilometers from Rome, but only 94 kilometers from Venice. [6] The province produced a lot of men such as Luigi. They became such capable *taiapiera* (stonemasons) that they created works intended not only for the town and the entire region, which is known as Friuli Venezia Giulia, but also for the rest of Italy as well. They were called the "Spizzapiera di Midùn." [7]

According to Italian émigrés living here in America, Friuli Venezia Giulia's villages and small towns are all old and full of character. The region is rich in history, cultural events, architecture and art, and the people are dignified, hardworking and trustworthy.

This is the stock that Luigi Del Bianco came from.

These days, however, that quaint character is being challenged by the times we live in. Hang gliding and parasailing competitions abound in Meduno, which has a population of just 1,701. [8] Though the patron saint of the little municipality is the Madonna di Me-

---

[6] www.ItalySquare.com.
[7] Mountain Community of West Friuli, 2007.
[8] www.Comuni-Italiani.it.

duno, a local hair stylist named Andreino Ferroli has turned his barbershop into a shrine dedicated to Luigi Del Bianco.

"I used to collect things from the First and Second World Wars," said Ferroli thru a translator. "In my barbershop I often spoke with my clients about those objects. My clients knew I loved to collect things, so I received carving tools such as scalpels and hammers," he continued.

"The fates brought to my ear the name of Luigi Del Bianco," explained Ferroili, who said that his interest ultimately became such a true passion that he installed a panel about Luigi on the outside of his barbershop's entrance door.

"My late aunt Elisabetta Del Bianco was related with the family of Luigi Del Bianco and often told me about this relative of hers," added Ferroli. But the only known people currently related to Luigi who are still residing in Meduno don't speak of any Elisabetta in their family.

Twin brothers, Gino and Rino Del Bianco, claim that Luigi was a second cousin of their mother. According to Rino's daughter, neither her father nor uncle remember anything particularly interesting regarding his life in Meduno. "He was born here, in the same home where my father Rino still lives," she said through a translator.

"We are really proud to know that someone from our land took part in such an extraordinary work as that one realized by Luigi," she continued.

"We Friulan people are very proud of Luigi Del Bianco," added Michele Bernardon, the 68-year- old head of the Museo Provinciale della Vita Contadina "Diogene Penzi" — Sezione Lavoro ed Emigrazione (Provincial Museum of Rural Life "Diogene Penzi" — Section of Work and Emigration) in Cavasso Nuovo, a municipality near Meduno. "For me, he is the icon of the audacious emigrant, hard worker and lover of his country."

The only facility in Northern Italy which is entirely dedicated to emigration, The Provincial Museum's work and emigration section has an exhibition area of 450 square meters. There are almost 600 pictures, documents, passports and working tools on display attesting to the migratory movements and places Friulian people went *gi pal mont* ("going around the world").

According to Bernardon, in The Province of Pordenone, the story of Luigi Del Bianco is considered representative of the Friulan emigration to other parts of the world. It would probably be considered the standard for which all Friulan emigration was measured if it weren't for the fact that Primo Carnera, the heavyweight boxer who became world champion on June 27 1933, at Madison Square Garden in Manhattan, also hailed from the area.

"Despite their different ages and professional interests they were able to establish a deep understanding," said Bernardon of the relationship between Carnera and Luigi. So good was the bond between the pair, and so long lasting was their friendship, that Luigi years later would make an exact mold of Carnera's hands; after all, at 6' 6" tall and 275 pounds, Carnera arguably possessed the biggest hands — and had the biggest physique — of any heavyweight champion who ever fought.

"Primo spent time with the rest of Luigi's family too," added Bernardon. "During his many trips to Italy, he usually rode a bike from the nearby Town of Sequals to Meduno. From there on he had to walk uphill until he was able to reach the first houses of Del Bianco's village.

"Luigi's father was living there and then he would usually go downhill with him to the local *trattoria* (an Italian-style eating establishment serving food and wine) where they enjoyed a meal of *baccalà* (dried or salted codfish)," continued Bernardon.

For his part, Bernardon says he has tried to spread the word about Luigi as best he can. "Until ten or 15 years ago few people, even in Friuli and Meduno, knew anything about Luigi's legendary achievements," he says. But thanks to the museum, he continued, "many people now know the deeds of this great sculptor."

Bernardon's own book, *Scalpellini e tagliapietre* (*Stone Masons and Stonecutters from Friuli in the Western World*), which last year was translated into English in Toronto, Canada, devotes a considerable amount of space to Del Bianco.

It is not surprising that Bernardon's book is being distributed in Toronto, considering the large number of Famee Furlane clubs in such Canadian cities as Toronto, Vancouver and Hamilton, as well as such Canadian provinces as Ontario.[9] The members of these clubs, whose goals were to have an organization where emigrants could gather socially in order to maintain, enjoy and promote their family values, culture and traditions, as well as be available to anyone needing help assimilating into Canadian society, all belong to the international society, *Ente Friuli nel Mondo*, a private non-profit organization founded in June 1953 that has satellite offices in Brazil and Argentina.[10] The society, which honored Luigi at its August 2008 convention, claims membership of some 22,000 individuals.

Lucy and Vincent Maraldo, of New Rochelle, New York, belong to the North America chapter, which is located in College Point, Queens and which honored Luigi at a testimonial dinner held in March 1992.

Not surprisingly, the Maraldos can't sing Luigi's praises enough. "He is another Friulan who has brought distinction to our community," said the couple in a handwritten letter to the author. "Luigi is an inspiration to today's generation by showing them that, by establishing your goals, persevering and working hard, you can achieve success."

---

[9] www.FameeFurlaneVancouver.com.
[10] www.friulinelmondo.com.

CHAPTER 2

BARRE

The single-family house sits on a 7,841-square-foot lot at 10 Sixth Street, in Barre, Vermont. Depending on whom you ask, its estimated value is currently $96,200, though similar homes in the neighborhood have sold for $95,000. According to Karen L. Dawes, who is the City Clerk and Treasurer of Barre, it was last sold on September 2, 2004 to Sergeant Paul Miscavage, a propulsion superintendent for the Vermont Air National Guard, and his wife, Patricia Lund-Miscavage.[11]

Though the house is fairly nondescript, as are most of the homes on Sixth Street, its former owner says the Miscavages have done a great job fixing it up. "The people we sold it to have done a nice job, they've spruced it up nicely," says Louis Joseph Cassani, who runs Barre Optical, the eye care center on North Main Street. Cassani's late father, Anthony, who died 14 years ago, grew up in that house, says his son. Prior to that, the home was owned by Cassani's grandfather, Luigi.

Dawes confirms for a reporter that Luigi Cassani owned the property in 1913. A professional storyteller named Lou Del Bianco, of Port Chester, New York, adds that Luigi used it as a boarding house.

This is news to the 60-year-old optician, who might as well be bug-eyed when he is first informed of this fact. "I never knew that," he says. And he says he certainly doesn't recall Anthony ever telling him that.

---

[11] Email to author, July 30, 2013.

"I remember going to visit my grandmother there, but I was very young at the time," he adds. "A boarding house, huh?" says the incredulous Cassani.

If only the walls of this house could talk, what a story they would tell. They would tell the story of one of Cassani's boarders, an immigrant stone cutter from Meduno, Italy named Luigi Del Bianco — Lou Del Bianco's grandfather.

Luigi traveled to Vienna, Austria when he was only 11-years-old to study stone carving. After studying in Venice for a time, the then-17-year-old Del Bianco came to America, where he settled in Barre.

According to *The Italian American Experience: An Encyclopedia*, the first Italian carvers to arrive in Barre came in 1880 from Carrara, which is a city in the Province of Massa, Italy; consequently, between 1880 and 1890, the marble industry in Barre experienced a huge uptick.[12]

Italian immigrants accounted for half of the town's population in 1910, according to Russ Joseph Morisi, an Adjunct Professor at the College of Staten Island.[13] Of the 12,000 people who lived in Barre at the outset of the 20th Century, he continues, 4,500 of them were working in the granite industry.[14] The granite that was quarried, cut and carved in 1910 accounted for up to 30 percent of all national production, he adds.[15]

Which explains why, even more than a century later, Barre's unofficial nickname is "The Granite Center of the World."

Barre Historical Society Librarian Paul Carnahan has precious little information about Luigi in his files. "Del Bianco wasn't here

[12] Salvatore J. LaGumina; Frank J. Cavaioli, Salvatore Primeggia and Joseph Varacalli, *The Italian American Experience; An Encyclopedia*, Garland Publishing, 1999.
[13] Russ Joseph Morisi, *A Socioeconomic Study Exploring the Immigration of Artisan Stone Cutters from Italy to the United States of America, Circa 1830-1920*, The College of Staten Island, 2009.
[14] Ibid.
[15] Ibid.

very long and didn't leave many tracks, as far as we can tell," says Carnahan, who does his due diligence and discovers that there is a Del Bianco listed in both the 1908 and 1911 City of Barre directories who worked for the Guidici Brothers and the World Granite companies.[16]

After returning to his homeland to fight for Italy during World War 1, Del Bianco emigrated back to Barre in 1920 to continue plying his trade. Eventually, he moved to Port Chester, New York, where he met a woman and fell in love.

It might have been the best thing he ever did professionally, since his future bride's brother-in-law subsequently introduced him to a friend of his in Stamford, Connecticut — one John Gutzon de la Mothe Borglum.

Del Bianco would carve out a niche for himself as one of Gutzon Borglum's most valued assistants, helping the famous sculptor throughout the 1920's on such projects as the Wars of America Memorial in Newark, New Jersey, among others.

Their best work, however, was yet to come.

In Barre, the name Del Bianco doesn't mean anything to the residents. Some of the city's most accomplished citizens haven't a clue as to who this man is.

"Nothing comes to mind," says Paul Heller, trustee of the Barre Historical Society and author of *Granite City Tales* (CreateSpace Independent Publishing Platform, 2012), his collected writings on the history of Barre.[17]

"I regret that I have no information about him," says Heller.[18]

Sue Higby, executive director of Studio Place Arts, a visual arts center on North Main Street, is asked if she's heard of Del Bianco. "I have a great deal of familiarity with living stone carvers in our region," she acknowledges. "However, I don't have any knowledge

---

[16] Email to author, July 2, 2013
[17] Email to author, July 9, 2013.
[18] Ibid.

about Mr. Del Bianco."[19]

Turns out, Del Bianco also resided at 565 North Main Street, but that house was torn down several years ago. As for Luigi Cassani, he seems to be an anomaly among people living in Barre who used their homes as boarding houses back then — according to Susan L. Richards, from 1880 to 1910, between 45 and 51 percent of Barre's working women earned income from taking in boarders.[20] Ethnically, she writes, these individuals were largely of Scottish and Italian descent.[21]

Sure, the same townsfolk know that a Luigi named Galleani was an anarchist who in 1906 founded a weekly propaganda paper in Barre called *Cronaca Sovversiva* (The Chronicle of Subversion),[22] and that Barre's original Primo Maggio celebration — the first great Italian rite of Spring that is celebrated every May 1st — was organized by Barre granite workers shortly after the Socialist Labor Hall opened in 1901.[23]

But ask them who was the chief carver of "The Shrine of Democracy" — the Mount Rushmore National Memorial — and they all draw a blank.

---

[19] Email to author, July 9, 2013.
[20] Susan L. Richards, Making Home Pay: Italian and Scottish Boardinghouse Keepers in Barre, 1880-1918, *Vermont History* 74, Vermont Historical Society, , Winter/Spring 2006.
[21] Ibid.
[22] "Luigi Galleani and the Anarchists of Barre," *Barre Montpelier Times Argus*, April 30, 2010.
[23] www.oldlaborhall.com.

CHAPTER 3

BUSTING WITH PRIDE

A 49 ½ pound bust of his grandfather occupies a prominent place in Lou's living room.

Thirteen inches tall, the 6 ½" by 9 inches marble sculpture of Luigi, who carved it of himself when he was a young man, is the sort of family heirloom you'd expect a family-oriented guy like Lou to display — hanging on a coat rack to the entrance of his house are both of the fedoras that Luigi used to wear when he took his regular walks around Washington Park in Port Chester.

"My grandfather was six feet tall and I am six foot four so the hat doesn't really fit me," concedes Lou. "But it's great to have nonetheless!"

Seeing it for the first time, a visitor to the Del Bianco household can't help but be impressed by the attention to detail that was obviously lavished on it. Mentioning that to Lou immediately triggers a tidal wave of memories.

"When I used to visit him at his apartment, I thought it was the most beautiful thing I had ever seen," recalls Lou, who was all of six when Luigi died. "When I walked into his bedroom every Sunday to greet him at his bedside, the contrast of seeing the 'young Luigi' and then the 'old Luigi' was never lost on me."

"My grandfather was very sick at this point in his life, so his physical strength wasn't there and his voice was raspy and weak from his diseased lungs. Still, he always managed to get out of bed and lead me to that bust. I would stand on a chair and feel that marble face with my six-year-old fingers."

"I have such pride and love for him, even though I only knew him for such a short time," adds Lou of Luigi, who died on January 20, 1969 of accelerated silicosis that was brought on, in part, by his not wearing a mask while working at the monument. "His lungs had turned to granite by the time he died," says Lou, ruefully.

Silicosis is the price one can pay for working around granite. For example, in an April 1970 issue of the *British Journal of Industrial Medicine,* researchers reported that the first case of silicosis in three decades was discovered in a granite quarry and crushing plant in Austria in 1958.[24]

Thirty years later, the *Rutland Herald* reported that the United States' Department of Health & Human Services' National Toxicology Program (NTP) concluded that the tiny crystalline rock particles found in granite dust could cause lung cancer.[25]

Citing studies that found elevated lung cancer rates among those working with stone and other products made from quartz or sand, the NTP listed crystalline silica dust as a known human carcinogen.[26]

As recently as May 2011, the *Journal of Occupational and Environmental Medicine* even reported on a University of Vermont study examining the relationships between silica exposure and mortality from lung cancer and other respiratory diseases.[27] The university's Department of Medical Biostatistics assessed more than 7,000 workers employed in the granite industry between 1947 and 1998 and found that mortality ratios were significantly elevated for lung cancer, tuberculosis and silicosis.[28]

Lou says that he only found out about his grandfather's work

---

[24] Grundorfer,W., and Raber, A., "Progressive Silicosis in Granite Workers," *British Journal of Industrial Medicine*, Volume 27, Issue 2.

[25] John Dillon, "Granite Dust," *Rutland Herald*, May 28, 2000.

[26] Ibid.

[27] Pamela Vacek; David Verma; William Graham, Peter Callas and Graham Gibbs, "Mortality in Vermont Granite Workers and its Association with Silica Exposure," *Journal of Occupational and Environmental Medicine*, Volume 68, No.5.

[28] Ibid.

on the monument by accident and only after he passed away.

"In 1971, I was eight years-old," says Lou, wiping away the tears. "And I discovered an old pamphlet about Mount Rushmore. When I asked my mother about it, she said, 'Oh, well Grandpa carved Lincoln's eyes.' And I said, 'What?' I was thunderstruck."

Without Luigi to bear witness to his work, Lou was bereft of any information about his grandfather's role in the creation of the monument. That's when he says he and his late Uncle Caesar made four trips to the Library of Congress in the 1980s to once and for all discover how important Luigi had been to the project.

"Even though most authors don't mention my grandfather, my uncle and I were able to 'find' Luigi through the most credible and reliable source there was — Gutzon Borglum himself," says Lou of those trips to Washington, D.C. "Borglum loved my grandfather and gave him the credit he deserved through his own writings. So, while Caesar and I started this journey together, I know he left this world confident that I would continue it."

Besides pure pride in his late grandfather, Lou says he has another reason to see to it that Luigi gets the credit he feels he is deserving of. Lambasting what he calls the pejorative image of Italian Americans, which reality shows such as "Mob Wives" and "Jersey Shore" help perpetuate, Lou says that Luigi "can be seen as a new, refreshing and positive symbol of what it means to be an Italian American.

"I have always been proud of my heritage, first and foremost, because of the great artists, musicians and scientists that came out of our culture," he explains. "Knowing that my grandfather was a great artist of that ilk who contributed to a world renowned sculpture is inspirational."

Luigi's official title was chief carver, so he was responsible for giving the monument its "refinement of expression," as Borglum himself characterized it. Essentially, Del Bianco did more than blast away at the granite to sculpt the four figures — he gave the monument its soul, as anyone who has looked into Lincoln's eyes can attest.

Vincent Chiarello, the former Public Affairs Adviser at the United States Embassy to the Holy See, appreciates where Lou is coming from. Chiarello, who says he once put his hands on the ceiling of the Sistine Chapel and actually handled the *conto* (bill) that Michelangelo Buonarroti submitted for the materials to paint it, used to advise the U.S. Ambassador on United States — Vatican diplomacy.[29]

"Del Bianco was not alone in executing his craft in the States," says Chiarello. Many of the men responsible for the stonework at the National Cathedral in Washington, D.C. were of Italian descent, he says, alluding to such individuals as Andrea and Emilio Cocozzella. "Yes, they were truly master craftsmen."[30]

Ermelindo Eduardo Ardolino is known for his work at the Cathedral of Saint John the Divine, in Manhattan, and Heinz Memorial Chapel, in Pittsburgh. Attilio and Furio Piccirilli carved Daniel Chester French's mammoth statue of Abraham Lincoln, at the Lincoln Memorial in Washington, D.C. But who knows of Luigi Del Bianco's work at Mount Rushmore?

---

[29] August 16, 2013 email to author.
[30] Ibid.

CHAPTER 4

"SILVIO, I HAVE A FEELING WE'RE NOT IN PORT CHESTER ANYMORE"

When work began at Mount Rushmore, it was actually another Italian immigrant and stone cutter named Hugo Villa who was the chief carver.

An accomplished sculptor in his own right, Villa was a great choice to be the head carver. Born in Roppolo, in northern Italy, in 1883, Villa grew up in the village of Ponderano. [31] A talented musician who played the violin and was also a violin maker, he studied sculpture at the Academy of Beaux Arts for one year while in Albertina.[32]

Among his works, he designed the statue of Henry Smith, the first American Governor of Texas, that sits in the West Coast Texas town of Brazoria.[33] He also was responsible for the Pioneer Monument in Landa Park, which is located in New Braunfels, Texas. Funded by German-Americans throughout Texas, the statue depicts a German immigrant pioneer family.[34]

After the partially completed bust of George Washington was unveiled, on July 4, 1930, Borglum assigned Villa to complete the carving of Washington. His next task was to be his undoing — the sculpting of Thomas Jefferson's face.[35]

In the book, *The Carving of Mount Rushmore*, author Rex Allen

---

[31] www.battersbyornamental.com.
[32] Ibid.
[33] www.texasescapes.com.
[34] www.sophienburg.com.
[35] Morisi, *A Socioeconomic Study Exploring the Immigration of Artisan Stone Cutters from Italy to the United States of America, Circa 1830-1920*, The College of Staten Island, 2009.

Smith notes that the process of sculpting Jefferson's head was to be "... a colossal disaster in the making."[36] According to Smith, Villa inspected the area where Jefferson's head was to be carved, and emerged with concerns about the inferior quality of the granite on that side of the mountain. But Borglum overruled Villa, who began to sculpt Jefferson at Borglum's instructions.[37]

Afterwards, Borglum was so upset with the way Jefferson's face turned out that his original vision of where Jefferson would be located on the mountain had to be jettisoned. For doing what he was told and heeding Borglum's directions, Villa was summarily fired.[38]

When Del Bianco was hired by Borglum in 1933 to replace Villa as chief carver, one of the first things he was instructed to do was dynamite the bust of Jefferson off the mountain before starting anew.

Two years later, Del Bianco brought his family out to the Black Hills of South Dakota to live with him in the town of Keystone.

Del Bianco's wife, Nicoletta Cardarelli, had misgivings about the trip almost from the get-go. For starters, in the days before interstate highways and commercial air travel, it usually took Luigi six days to make the drive from Port Chester to South Dakota, according to a published account.[39]

In a 1933 letter that Borglum's wife, Mary, sent to Luigi, he is advised to make the trip by car by going via Philadelphia.[40] Mrs. Borglum estimated that the cost of the journey would be $75 for maintenance of the vehicle, and $40 for gas.[41]

Perhaps more significantly, Nicoletta was concerned that leav-

---

[36] Rex Alan Smith, *The Carving of Mount Rushmore*, Abbeville Press Publishers, 1985.
[37] Ibid.
[38] Morisi, *A Socioeconomic Study Exploring the Immigration of Artisan Stone Cutters from Italy to the United States of America, Circa 1830-1920*, The College of Staten Island, 2009.
[39] Yvette Kahn, "Luigi Del Bianco and Mount Rushmore: A Monumental Job," *Village Views*, Summer 1991.
[40] Ibid.
[41] Ibid.

ing for Keystone meant uprooting her three young children — Caesar, Vincent and Silvio — from Port Chester and taking them cross country to a place where Italian Americans were not exactly found in abundance.

Even today, Italian Americans represent only one percent of the total population of South Dakota, according to the United States Census Bureau. Only 714 people reside in Keystone and, of those, less than one percent — 0.75% — classify themselves as Italian Americans.[42]

According to the United States Census Bureau, there were about 5,000 identifiable Italian immigrants in the United States in 1850.[43] Over the next three decades, a total of 64,361 Italians immigrated to America.[44] Political upheaval in their homeland is generally given as the reason why they up and left their native soil.

For whatever the reason, over 5 million Italians immigrated to this country during the period 1875-1930, according to *The Immigrant Upraised*.[45] While Alexandra Elliott, of Villanova University, puts the numbers of Italians arriving in the United States from 1890 to 1900 at 655,888, two-thirds of whom were men,[46] Joan Rapczynski reports that, for the 40 year period between 1880 and 1920, 4 million Italians emigrated to this country.[47] Further, Dominic Candeloro notes that, between 1900 and 1910, 2 million Italians emigrated to the United States.[48] Based on U.S. Census Bureau data, he continues, the numbers peaked at 285,000 in 1907, 284,000 in

[42] www.zipatlas.com.

[43] United States Department of Commerce, Bureau of the Census, *Census of Population*.

[44] www.clevelandmemory.org.

[45] Andrew F. Rolle, *The Immigrant Upraised: Italian Adventurers and Colonists in an Expanding America*, University of Oklahoma Press, 1970.

[46] Alexandra Elliott, "The Immigration Essay," The Little Italy Lodge, Baltimore, Maryland.

[47] Joan Rapczynski, "The Italian Immigrant Experience in America (1870-1920), Yale-New Haven Teachers Institute.

[48] Dominic Candeloro, "Italian Americans," *Multiculturalism in the United States: A Comparative Guide to Acculturation and Ethnicity*, Greenwood Press, 2005.

1914, and 222,000 in 1921.[49]

As with most groups who came to these shores, the lure of a better life most likely spurred them to leave their homeland.

In spite of the numbers of Italian immigrants coming to the United States, most didn't choose to put down stakes in South Dakota. The immigrants who did choose South Dakota were mostly Norwegian, with a smattering of Czech but, in actuality, the most widespread of all the ethnic groups to South Dakota were the Germans.[50]

In *Dakota Resources: A Preliminary Guide for Studying Ethnic Groups in South Dakota*, Gerald F. DeJong examines in excruciating detail the Fourteenth Census of the United States. He found that, in 1920, of South Dakota's total population of 636,547, just 82,574 (13%) were foreign born.[51]

Of those 82,574, 413 individuals identified themselves as Italian.[52] Care to guess how many Italians settled in Pennington County, where Keystone is?

All of thirteen.[53]

No, if you were an Italian immigrant in South Dakota, the place to go was Lawrence County — more than 50 percent (262) of all the Italians living in the state in 1920 settled there.[54]

So you can just imagine Nicoletta's reaction upon arriving in South Dakota; like Dorothy Gale, who found herself asking her dog, Toto, where they were after a tornado thrust them both out of the Kansas plains and deposited them in Munchkinland, the matriarch of the Del Bianco family might have turned to one of her

---

[49] Ibid.
[50] Rex C. Myers, *An Immigrant Heritage: South Dakota's Foreign Born in the Era of Assimilation,* South Dakota State Historical Society, 1989.
[51] Gerald F. DeJong, *Dakota Resources: A Preliminary Guide for Studying Ethnic Groups in South Dakota,* South Dakota State Historical Society, 1985.
[52] Ibid.
[53] Ibid.
[54] Ibid.

sons and exclaimed, "Silvio, I have a feeling we're not in Port Chester, anymore."

But it was more than just finding a fellow lansman to relate to. According to the Keystone Historical Society, Nicolletta experienced culture shock almost immediately when she discovered that the rental house where they lived, behind the Keystone Trading Post, didn't have indoor plumbing. Also, she was unable to buy the necessary ingredients at the Keystone Trading Company to prepare the family's favorite Italian dishes. The family never returned after 1935 and, starting that year, Luigi roomed and boarded in a boarding house at the foot of Mount Rushmore during his remaining time in the Black Hills.

The above information came directly from the website of the Keystone Area Historical Society, whose president, Sandy McLain, told the author in an email that her group didn't know anything about Del Bianco. "Bob (Hayes) put the information on the site without our permission."[55]

Hayes's father, Edwald, used to hoist men up to the faces on cable cars.

Interestingly, only one week after receiving her email, the author noted that all references to Luigi had been stricken from the website entirely.

Due to a lack of funding, work at the monument came to screeching halts quite often. Even Lincoln Borglum admits that his father grossly underestimated the costs of the project. In *Mount Rushmore: The Story Behind the Scenery*, Lincoln writes that Gutzon estimated that the memorial would cost about $400,000 and take four years to complete.[56] As it turned out, the project actually cost just a shade under $1 million ($989,992.32 to be exact) and work

---

[55] September 13, 2013 email to author..

[56] Lincoln Borglum, *Mount Rushmore: The Story Behind the Scenery*, KC Publications, 1993.

was done sporadically over a span of 14 years.[57]

In his father's defense, Lincoln argued that there was no real way of knowing how much the project would actually cost, because there was no comparable work on which to base estimates.

The shutdowns prompted Del Bianco to quit twice, first in 1935, and then five years later, in 1940. Otherwise, he stayed six months at a time in South Dakota.

For his efforts, Luigi was reportedly paid $1.50 an hour, or $72 per week.[58] With the notable exception of Villa, who received $20 per day — Borglum personally defrayed half of that amount — nobody else ever earned more.

As for Lou's uncles, their experiences were apparently far more pleasant than their mother's. "I remember the general store in town and a bar across the street which had a boxing ring in the back," Caesar wrote years later. "Even today I found it humorous and strange that there was a boxing ring there."

The children of the workers all attended school in the one-room Keystone Schoolhouse, which is now occupied by the Keystone Historical Museum. Years later, the adult Vincent would fondly recall his days in Keystone, and the friendships the Del Biancos made with the Lakota Indians.

"My brothers and I (the oldest Del Bianco child, Theresa, had died at the age of four from meningitis, while one other daughter Gloria, had not been born yet) were at their reservation all the time, cutting our fingers and becoming blood brothers with them," he told reporter Yvette Kahn in 1991. "My father became a blood brother with their chief."[59]

"One of the reasons they all got along so well was that they were all foreigners," says Lou, who was the third youngest of Vin-

---

[57] Ibid.
[58] Kahn, "Luigi Del Bianco and Mount Rushmore: A Monumental Job," *Village Views*, Summer 1991.
[59] Ibid.

cent's seven children but his only son. "The Indians were foreign-ers and so was my grandfather."

"I saw the house where I lived, the stream where I went fishing, the woods where I played and that old schoolhouse," said Vincent, who went back to the Black Hills in July 1991 to celebrate the 50th anniversary of Mount Rushmore. "It was very moving."[60]

More moving was footage that Gloria herself recorded in 1991, during the 50th anniversary celebration of the monument, which is part of the website, www.luigimountrushmore.com, that Lou cre-ated in 2010 to honor his grandfather. In it, Gloria by accident meets a then 86-year-old man named George Rumple — who served as the foreman at Mount Rushmore because Borglum liked the fact that he was a stone carver too. In the home movie, Rumple extols Del Bianco's many talents.

"He wasn't just a stone cutter, he was a genius," says Rumple of Luigi. "He taught me lots of things, he gave me lots of good advice and he could have easily taken Borglum's place if Lincoln hadn't been there.

"Borglum should have doubled his salary," continues Rumple, who says he affectionately referred to Del Bianco as 'L Del.' "I learned more than a few pointers from him, let me tell you. I can't praise him enough, he was a very gifted artist."

George Rumple passed away not too long after meeting 'L Del's' daughter at that 50th anniversary celebration.

---

[60] Ibid.

Luigi in Barre, VT, circa 1913

CHAPTER 5

"IT'S LIKE TALKING ABOUT THE '36 YANKEES AND NOT MENTIONING JOE DIMAGGIO"

History has not treated Luigi Del Bianco very kindly. For instance, in Smith's book, Del Bianco is not mentioned *once* — and Smith's work is widely considered to be the definitive book on the artistic and engineering dynamics that went into the creation of Mount Rushmore.

Interestingly, though Villa is included in Smith's book, he is not mentioned in Gilbert C. Fite's seminal *Mount Rushmore*, according to Rod Evans, a portrait artist in Sioux Falls, South Dakota who says he met Smith in 1993 at a reception in Keystone for his musical play, *Road To Rushmore*.[61]

Evans, who mistakenly believed that Villa had also been omitted from *The Carving of Mount Rushmore*, could only conjecture as to why Rushmore's first chief carver was excised from Fite's book. "Perhaps it was because Villa was (unjustly) fired so early in the Rushmore project," wrote Evans in an email to the author.[62]

In his book's foreword, Smith writes that "the story of Mount Rushmore Memorial is not a simple story of a sculptor and a mountain."[63] In that respect, he couldn't have been more spot on. Funding for the project was always at issue, and work on the monument was frequently halted due to lack of monies. The fact that there were not many trained men seasoned in the art of carving and sculpture also bogged down work on the memorial.

---

[61] August 28, 2013 email to the author.
[62] Ibid.
[63] Smith, *The Carving of Mount Rushmore*, Abbeville Press, 1985.

Robert E. Hayes — whose information about Luigi was taken off the website of the Keystone Historical Society — wrote his own book about the monument. In *Mount Rushmore and Keystone*, Hayes' take on the history of the local area, he pays special attention to the effect that the monument had on Keystone, especially with regards to tourism. He, too, acknowledges early on that "Borglum could not, of course, carve the mountain alone, yet other professional sculptors were not available."[64]

Contacted via telephone in September 2013, the retired mining engineer and octogenarian writer — who attended school with Vincent Del Bianco — was asked how he could write that sentence knowing that both Del Bianco and Villa were clearly professional sculptors.

"I was limited to what I could write," he explained. "The publisher didn't want everything I had written."

Arcadia Press published *Mount Rushmore and Keystone* in 2006 as part of its "Images of America" series.

Asked to comment about Hayes's explanation, Arcadia Publisher Maggie Bullwinkel essentially agreed with him. She told the author in a September 2013 email that "our books are local and regional pictorial histories and are not intended to be comprehensive histories of any place or landmark.[65]

"As part of the 'Images of America' series, Mr. Hayes had to work within a specific format that allows approximately 200 images and captions within 128 pages," she continued. "He also had to work with the images available to him."[66]

Hayes's father, Edwald, had been the hoist engineer on Mount Rushmore, "so when I was a boy my mother and I used to pack lunches and go spend the day there," he recalls. "And I remember seeing my Dad hoist as many as five men at a time up on the tram-

---

[64] Robert E. Hayes, *Mount Rushmore and Keystone*. Arcadia Publishing, 2006.
[65] September 16, 2013 email to author.
[66] Ibid.

way to the faces.

"I grew up at Mount Rushmore," he continues. "And even though the tram was full, the workers always let me ride up with them, I suppose 'cause I was a little guy."

According to Hayes, Borglum hosted many a dinner for the workers at the boarding house near the monument or at the Alex Johnson Hotel in Rapid City. He even threw picnics at his Hermosa ranch, continued Hayes.[67]

"As part of the Mount Rushmore family, I attended many of the parties." he said. "I especially remember the Christmas of 1940 in the old studio building at Rushmore, where Dad played Santa Claus."[68]

Those nostalgic boyhood memories vanish quickly for Hayes when he is asked point blank if he remembers whether Del Bianco was ever the butt of any anti-Italian jokes.

"No, nothing like that at all," he said. "We were a small community."

Apparently, if Hayes's way of thinking is to be taken as gospel, bigots and prejudiced people can only be found in large, urban cities.

✳ ✳ ✳

"There are only two mistakes one can make along the road to truth," according to Buddha. "Not going all the way and not starting."

It was the simple failure of Smith's book to mention Del Bianco that started Lou and his late uncle, Caesar, on the journey to champion Luigi's contributions and rewrite history.

For his book, Smith interviewed many of the men who actually worked on the mountain. But when Luigi's son, Caesar, read the

---

[67] Robert E. Hayes, "Borglum's Last Christmas," *South Dakota Magazine*, July-August 2006.
[68] Ibid.

book and discovered that his father hadn't been interviewed, he almost blew a gasket, according to Lou.

"He told me, 'It's like talking about the 1936 New York Yankees and not mentioning Joe DiMaggio,'" recalls Lou. "My Uncle Caesar was very passionate about his Papa's contribution to Mount Rushmore, and very serious about the serious omission of his father from many of the published books about Rushmore."

So Caesar and Lou set out three times, in 1989, 1990 and 1991, for our nation's capital to discover for themselves the exact role that Luigi played in the carving of Mount Rushmore.

"If I remember correctly, Louis and I left rather early, around 5 A.M," wrote Caesar years later. "It was a nice trip and we had plenty of (Frank) Sinatra tapes."

What they found was a real eye-opener, according to Lou.

"Caesar hit the motherload," he says. "He found amazing stuff."

In the Library of Congress's manuscript division, Caesar found the collected papers of Gutzon Borglum. All told, there were approximately 190 boxes of information, covering Borglum's life and career.

Thirty of these boxes were just about Mount Rushmore.

"You have no idea how excited I was anticipating what I would find in them," wrote Caesar. "It was such a great feeling to find letters, memos, etc., all about my father."

"Caesar continued to make great finds with every trip we made to D.C. together," says Lou. "This research was the highlight of his life."

Borglum's papers put to rest once and for all any lingering doubt of the important role that Luigi played in the carving of Mount Rushmore.

When he died in 2009, Caesar told his nephew that he was now passing the torch to him, that it would be Lou's job to get Luigi the credit that he hadn't received.

"You have to take over Rushmore now," Lou says Caesar told

him.

And that's exactly what Lou's been doing.

* * *

When Smith passed away in October 2010, a National Park Service (NPS) official called his book required reading for all new Mount Rushmore tour guides.[69]

"It's a critical part of the education of our front-line interpreters," Bruce Weisman, curator and chief of resource management at Mount Rushmore, told the *Rapid City Journal* in 2010. "Rex's book is certainly the first one we start with."[70]

"We don't have that firsthand experience anymore," continued Weisman. "But through the book, we were able to gain some of those experiences. In terms of the carving history, it's really quite an exceptional piece."[71]

"Rex Allen Smith's book is considered the bible of the building of the mountain," agreed Tina Nichols Curry, whose own book, *Hanging Off Jefferson's Nose; Growing Up on Mount Rushmore*, is about Borglum's son, Lincoln.[72]

Smith's book continues to be sold at the visitor's center at Mount Rushmore, and Weisman said at the time of his passing that "it will always be the case.[73]

"It is a big loss to South Dakota," Weisman continued, referring to Smith's death. "His book was an enormous contribution to the history of Mount Rushmore."[74]

According to Lou, early in 2011 he contacted Weisman directly. Weisman, he says, "loved Luigi's story and did everything he could" to ensure that "I'd be able to actually perform my one-man

---

[69] *Rapid City Journal*, October 7, 2010.
[70] Ibid.
[71] Ibid.
[72] August 26, 2013 email to author.
[73] *Rapid City Journal*, October 7, 2010.
[74] Ibid.

show in the sculptor's studio."

A five-time Parent's Choice Award winner who has been doing a 45-minute one-man show about Luigi's life and work, "In the Shadow of the Mountain," before school-age audiences and fraternal groups, among others, for the last three years, Lou says he was then put in touch with Blaine Kortemeyer, who was at that time the acting Chief of Interpretation.

"Blaine saw a video of my one-man show and we talked about Mount Rushmore flying me out to the mountain and giving me an honorarium to do some performances," explains Lou, "but at the last minute, Mount Rushmore reneged and told me there was no money in the budget to do something like that."

So Lou and his wife, Camille Linen, drove to South Dakota in order to do five shows. And he performed them all for free, on July 3, 2011.

"It was surreal," says Lou, who added that standing in the same studio where his grandfather had worked on models of the presidential faces "was just a more profound experience for me than I ever thought it was going to be."

"On the day of the performances, Camille and I didn't know what to expect," Lou says. "We were really going in cold! How would total strangers take to this new story? After all, there was no lead up to my visit and being a non celebrity, would people really care that much? Would they be moved or touched by Luigi's story and my portrayal as him?

"I know it was 2011," says Lou, "but having heard a tourist the day before talk about having 'a good, dago, guinea meal,' I wondered whether some people from the heartland would reject the story of some "guinea", some "I-talian"? Or the gentleman who told me when he saw the way I looked he asked, 'Are you from around here? I don't think so.'

"When I got out of the van, a young park ranger came running up to me. He looked like a little kid on Christmas day," continues

Lou. "'Hi, my name is Dustin (Baker, the Sculptor in Residence) , and I am so excited to meet you! I read so much about your grandfather and I can't wait to see the show. What an amazing guy!' I shook Dustin's hand, thanked him, and realized with great relief that people were starving for this kind of story. I knew now it was going to be a very special day.

"After the performance, the audience would not stop clapping," recalls Lou. "There was no resistance at all. No rolling eyes at when I played Luigi, with his funny accent and colorful personality. It was, in fact, a total embracing of Luigi the artist, finally getting recognized for his talent and hard work. Several Park Rangers came up to me afterwards and said, 'Wow! I had no idea about your grandfather. This is incredible! Can I use parts of your show in my walking tour? I said, 'Are you kidding me? That would be the best thing anyone could ask me today!'"

"After my interview with a local newspaper, Camille and I went to the main observation deck to see the sculpture one more time," says Lou. "We started a conversation with a couple from Washington State who came to the mountain on motorcycle. I started telling them about Luigi and as usual, their eyes lit up. 'Really? That is fantastic!,' they told us.

"Right after that, a hand tapped me on the shoulder." says Lou. "It was a cute little lady who burst out, 'I just heard about your grandfather! They said he was Borglum's right hand man and that the mountain wouldn't be the same without him!' The park rangers were already at work, spreading Luigi's story to the masses. Then this sweet little woman from the Midwest wanted to be in a photo with the grandson of Luigi. There was no hint of 'the other.' Or 'the I-talian.' Or 'the outsider.' There was only Luigi, the chief carver, the artist. I couldn't have ended my trip to Rushmore in a better way."

However, three years later, Weisman was no longer curator at the memorial. But Maureen McGee-Ballinger was the Chief of Interpretation & Education.

Lou says that, subsequent to his five performances at Mount Rushmore, Superintendent Cheryl Schreier indicated that she was amenable to a permanent exhibit honoring Luigi.

However, after submitting his proposal, Lou claims Ballinger told him it was way too ambitious for Mount Rushmore, and that the notion of a Luigi Del Bianco exhibit would have to go on the "back burner," to be part of long range planning for the future.

Schreier backs up Ballinger.[75] Contacted via email, Schreier confirmed that Lou had indeed submitted a formal proposal about a permanent exhibition honoring Luigi, but begged off from commenting further. "Unfortunately at this time we do not have the resources to address any changes for our permanent exhibits and long range interpretive planning would need to occur before any changes were implemented."[76]

Contacted via email and asked whether she thought Weisman's statements about Smith's book was somewhat flawed, given the fact that it failed to mention Del Bianco at all, McGee-Ballinger danced around the question like a *prima ballerina assoluta* in her response to the author: "Luigi Del Bianco was one of the skilled carvers that traveled from the East to work on the sculpture." she replied.[77] "While many workers were learning on the job, Mr. Del Bianco, Hugo Villa, William S. Tallman and Joseph Bruner, all of whom studied under Gutzon Borglum in the East, were all skilled craftsman who contributed to the sculpture. All of them joined in the massive undertaking that became the sculpture we know today."

"Mr. Del Bianco is recognized for his contributions to the sculpture both in our museum and on our Workers Wall," she continued. "His work is also noted in publications sold in the park bookstore."[78]

---

[75] September 24, 2013 email to author.
[76] Ibid.
[77] August 23, 2013 email to author.
[78] Ibid.

Asked whether she thought it was inspirational that an Italian immigrant to this country had served as the chief carver on such a renown, worldwide sculpture, McGee-Ballinger declined to respond altogether.

✳ ✳ ✳

Morisi doesn't mention Del Bianco either in his thoroughly researched master's thesis, *A Socioeconomic Study Exploring the Immigration of Artisan Stone Carvers from Italy to the United States Circa 1830-1920.* But at least he owned up to the omission.

"I just never came across any information on Luigi," acknowledges Morisi. "But I wasn't really surprised," he continues. "Stone carvers were never credited for anything."

Not that Luigi sought any credit. According to Gloria Del Bianco, her father wasn't a publicity hound. In an interview that aired on National Public Radio on October 27, 2011, Gloria remarked that "You know, my father did not talk about Mount Rushmore that much. He was a very modest man."

In that respect, Luigi was the polar opposite of Don "Nick" Clifford, who for years has billed himself as the only known individual still alive who worked at Mount Rushmore.

In actuality, as of last year, Clifford was one of only two individuals still alive who worked at Mount Rushmore who were witnesses to history.

In May 1938, Elwood "Whitey" Iverson was beginning a new job that he got courtesy of the Civilian Conservation Corps (CCC), the program which celebrated its 80th anniversary in 2013. The Emergency Conservation Work Act, the measure that established the CCC, was signed into law by President Franklin Roosevelt on March 31, 1933 as part of the New Deal.

A native of South Dakota who grew up on a farm, where his chores typically consisted of putting up fencing, taking care of livestock and cultivating corn, Iverson had no idea what he'd be doing

In the Finch interview, Clifford says he pestered Lincoln Borglum to hire him.[85]

"They hired me because I was a good baseball player," said Clifford, who was an outfielder and pitcher. "I knew how to run a jackhammer, too. I had learned in the mines down in Keystone. But they wanted a winning baseball team."[86]

According to the Rapid City Convention & Visitors Bureau, Mount Rushmore sponsored a baseball team that played other regional teams.[87] Gutzon and Lincoln Borglum were so competitive that they would hire workers just because they could play baseball. Though a majority of the new hires could swing a bat, they had no idea how to use the jackhammers or dynamite used to carve the mountain.[88]

In the Carvers Café at Mount Rushmore, the Memorial Team Ice Cream station is named in honor of the baseball team formed by the Mount Rushmore carvers. Life-size pictures of the carvers in their baseball uniforms are on the walls near the station.[89]

Clifford self-published his own book, *Mount Rushmore Q&A,* which he routinely sells and autographs for tourists when they come to the gift shops at Mount Rushmore.[90] And he has been a *de facto* good will ambassador for both the attraction and the Mount Rushmore Society — the fund-raising organization that operates the Mount Rushmore Bookstores, Mount Rushmore Audio Tour and the Mount Rushmore Institute.[91] The Society also operates the parking facility at Mount Rushmore under a concessions contract with the Park Service.[92]

---

[85] Ibid.
[86] Ibid.
[87] www.visitrapidcity.com.
[88] Ibid.
[89] "New Restaurant Greets Visitors," *Rapid City Journal,* April 23, 2006.
[90] www.mountrushmorecarver.com .
[91] www.mountrushmoresociety.com.
[92] Ibid.

The Society has a somewhat symbiotic relationship with the Park Service. According to the Summer 2013 issue of *Granite Journal*, which is the official newspaper of the Mount Rushmore National Memorial, the Society's history with the memorial dates back to 1930, when private funds were actively solicited for the project.[93] The Society raised $25 million in the 1990s to help fund $56 million in facility improvements, including that $17 million parking facility.[94]

According to the newsletter, the Society continues to be an active partner with the National Park Service:

> The Mount Rushmore Bookstores, celebrating 20 years in the park in 2013, contribute more than $150,000 to the park annually;

> The Society donated $35,000 in support of the summer Evening Lighting Ceremony. The money was used to open the season two weeks early and extend the season two additional weeks in 2013;

> The Society gave Mount Rushmore National Memorial $100,000 to be used for the preservation of the sculptures last year. This is the first of five $100,000 gifts that the Society is giving to the park over the next five years. The funds are a result of an initial $214,000 bequest from the estate of the late Betty Nelson that the Society has invested, contributed to and managed over the years. [95]

> The Society has raised more than half of a $396,000 goal to construct a permanent Youth Exploration Area so that children can experience engaging programs in a hands-on atmosphere.[96]

---

[93] *Granite Journal*, Mount Rushmore National Memorial, National Park Service, United States Department of the Interior, Summer 2013.
[94] Ibid.
[95] Ibid.
[96] Ibid.

When the Gutzon Borglum Memorial Highway Sign was re-dedicated in June 2013, both Clifford and his wife, Carolyn, as well as Society President Andy Knight and Executive Director Diana Saathoff were present at the ceremonies.[97] The South Dakota Department of Transportation had designated a 10-mile segment of Highway 22, between the 16A Junction near Keystone and the intersection with 385 south of Hill City, as the Borglum Memorial Highway, four decades earlier.[98]

Clifford is proud of the monument and the work he did on it, and has clearly enjoyed his more than 15 minutes of fame. So that is why it is so surprising that he seemingly lashed out at the Del Biancos after Gloria went on NPR three years ago with her nephew, Lou.

"I am the only known person, still living, who worked on Mt. Rushmore," he wrote after listening to the telecast.[99] "The records show Del Bianco worked in 1933, 1935, 1936, and 1937, not most of the 14 years it took to carve the monument.[100]

"I knew Luigi and many of the good carvers, some worked 10, 12, even all 14 years." he continued. "Luigi was a good carver, but his family does not have accurate information on some of their stories. I want to set the record straight."[101]

First, given all the stops and starts caused by the persistent lack of project funding, nobody has ever claimed that it took 14 years to sculpt the monument. More likely what Clifford meant to say is that, over a span of 14 years, total work actually amounted to six or seven years.

In *Mount Rushmore: The Story Behind the Scenery*, no less than

---

[97] *Rapid City Journal*, June 2, 2013.
[98] Ibid.
[99] "A Stone Carver's Daughter Tells of Mount Rushmore," National Public Radio, October 27, 2011.
[100] Ibid.
[101] Ibid.

Lincoln Borglum notes the project was shut down for a total of 7 1/2 of those 14 years for lack for funding. Sometimes, he continued, the project was shut down for two to three months at a time, sometimes six months or longer.[102]

Second, Del Bianco was not just a good carver — he was the *chief carver*. And he was a trained sculptor to boot, even being recognized by the National Sculpture Society in 1956.[103]

In a June 1933 letter to John Boland, chairman of the Mount Rushmore National Memorial Commission, Borglum notes how important Del Bianco was to the project:

> In 1932 I went without any (able-trained men) at all, placed Villa in charge of the work, and paid him personally half of his $20.00 a day, attempting by the close supervision of a semi-artist to overcome the absence of trained stone men. The experiment was not successful. You have got to have brains and knowledge in the fingers handling the drills. That is training.[104]

> (Del Bianco) entirely out-classed everyone on the hill, and his knowledge was an embarrassment to their amateur efforts and lack of knowledge, lack of experience and lack of judgment. He is the only man besides myself who has been on the work who knows the problems and how to instantly solve them.[105]

And, in a 1936 letter, Borglum described Del Bianco as "the only intelligent, efficient stone carver on the work who understands the language of the sculptor."[106]

Why would Clifford go out of his way to knock the Del Biancos? Was it petty jealousy on his part? Perhaps, but since Clifford has repeatedly failed to return the voice mail messages that the au-

---

[102] L. Borglum, *Mount Rushmore: The Story Behind the Scenery,* KC Publications, 1993.
[103] National Sculpture Society, September 28, 1956.
[104] Gutzon Borglum Papers, Manuscript Division, Library of Congress, Washington, D.C.
[105] Ibid.
[106] Ibid.

thor has left for him on the telephone, as well as the letter he was mailed, we might never know the reason for his animus.

Not to be outdone, on at least one occasion, Carolyn Clifford, has followed in her husband's footsteps, taking a pot shot at the South Dakota Department of Tourism for using mascots of the four presidents to promote tourism in the state.

In an item appearing on the department's own website, in May 2013, film and media representative Katlyn Richter notes that mascots representing the presidents enshrined on the Mount Rushmore National Memorial would embark on a 14-city tour across the Midwest, beginning May 23:

> The official tour by the presidential mascots and an accompanying street team from the Department of Tourism are part of the Department's Your American Journey marketing campaign. The campaign encourages vacationers to visit places of great historic significance, unimagined beauty and patriotic inspiration within the borders of South Dakota. The group will ride in style in a bus wrapped with custom artwork depicting the variety that South Dakota offers travelers.[107]

> "All of the cities along this tour are filled with people who have a high propensity to travel to South Dakota," says Jim Hagen, Secretary of the Department of Tourism. "The goal of the presidential mascots' tour is to build awareness about South Dakota, create excitement among those who see them, and plant the seed of a South Dakota vacation with all of the potential visitors we have the opportunity to speak with one-on-one."

> The mascots, designed to depict the mountain carving in the Black Hills, have traveled across the country the past two years, including a stop in New York City to watch the Mount Rush-

---

[107] "Presidential Mascots Bus Tour," *South Dakota Traveler,* May 17, 2013, South Dakota Department of Tourism.

more's American Pride float in the Macy's Thanksgiving Day Parade.[108]

Fairly innocuous stuff, right? Not according to Mrs. Clifford. In a comment she posted on the department's website shortly thereafter, she wrote:

> It is a disgrace that now our Dept. of Tourism is using ugly monsters, i.e. mascots, to advertise our beautiful National Memorial. Mount Rushmore is not a comical place to visit — many people are moved to tears when they see it for the first time. To paint these grotesque faces on the side of a bus, which goes around the region, instead of a photo of the real Shrine of Democracy shows that you folks in the Dept. of Tourism have no idea what this Memorial really means. Mascots are also an insult to the men who worked on Mt. Rushmore. My husband is Don 'Nick' Clifford who is the last living person who worked on the mountain carving. You are using ugly mascots of our United States Presidents to advertise a National Memorial, which is disrespectful. It is unbelievable and very disappointing! Please reconsider your advertising in the future and stop cheapening Mount Rushmore National Memorial.[109]

In response to Clifford's comments, Wanda Goodman, Deputy Media Secretary for the South Dakota Department of Tourism, replied that, while she certainly respected Mrs. Clifford's opinions, "I simply disagree with them."[110]

To his credit, Clifford, who grew up in Keystone, and who still owns a home there with Carolyn, donated to the memorial in 1996 what is often referred to as the Rushmore Workers Marker — a plaque recognizing and paying tribute to the nearly 400 individuals

---

[108] Ibid.
[109] www.blog.travelsd.com. June 18, 2013.
[110] In a September 4, 2013 email to the author.

who worked at the monument. For the record, Luigi Del Bianco's name is included as part of the plaque.

* * *

Robin Borglum Carter acknowledges that Park Service policy is to treat all the people who worked on the monument as a group, regardless of their titles or contributions. In a telephone interview with the author, the daughter of Lincoln Borglum (and grand-daughter of Gutzon Borglum) says that it was because her father and grandfather were the only two people *commissioned* by the federal government to do the work that they are the only ones the Park Service singles out.

According to Amy Bracewell, the former historian and educa-tion coordinator for Mount Rushmore National Memorial, "Luigi Del Bianco was one of many assistants to Borglum. Gutzon Bor-glum invited many of his colleagues and co-workers from his home studio in Connecticut to join him on his Mount Rushmore project. Some of them stayed on for a short time and some remained in-volved in the project for many years. Mr. Del Bianco was one of these artists that joined Borglum from their time in Connecticut. One of the history publications sites at least four or five of these artisans that Borglum invited to the project."[111]

"This is all I know of Mr. Del Bianco's involvement with the project," added Bracewell in an email she wrote prior to becoming the new site manager for Cedar Creek and Belle Grove National Historical Park, in Virginia. "His name is not coming up in my searches of our archives or Borglum's papers."[112]

However, Borglum's papers in the Library of Congress in Washington, D.C. tell a far different story. In them, it is clear how much he valued Luigi's, or as he affectionately called him, "Bian-co's," work. For instance, here is an entry dated June 3, 1933:

---

[111] In a February 12, 2013 email to the author.
[112] Ibid.

Bianco has all of Villa's ability plus power and honesty and dependability. We could double our progress if we could have two like Bianco.[113]

And here is an entry dated July 30, 1935:

All drilling of all kinds, roughing, finishing and carving of features must be directed by the chief stone carver and his directions followed. The chief carver will be held responsible for the ways and the means for removing and finishing the sculpture.... I have appointed Luigi Bianco for this most important task.[114]

In one of the only books that does heap well deserved praise on him, Judith St. George's *The Mount Rushmore Story*, Luigi is credited with single-handedly saving the face of Jefferson.[115] "He patched the crack in Jefferson's lip with a foot deep piece of granite held in place by pins — the only patch on the whole sculpture, and one that is hard to detect even close up," writes St. George, who subsequently notes that, "with the exception of Luigi Del Bianco, few of the carvers worked out."[116]

He also carved the life-like eyes of Abraham Lincoln. In a 1966 interview, Luigi told the *Yonkers Herald Statesman* that "the eye of Lincoln had to look just right from many miles distant. I know every line and ridge, each small bump and all the details of that head so well."[117]

"He was more than a worker, that's obvious," says Lou of his grandfather's unique contributions to Mount Rushmore. "Why can't the Park Service see that?"

Howard Shaff, who along with his wife, Audrey, authored *Six*

[113] Gutzon Borglum Papers, Manuscript Division, Library of Congress, Washington, D.C.
[114] Ibid.
[115] Judith St. George, *The Mount Rushmore Story*, G.P. Putnam's Sons, 1985.
[116] Ibid.
[117] "He Carved the Face of History," *Yonkers Herald Statesman*, May 14, 1966.

Wars at a Time; The Life and Times of Gutzon Borglum, understands the reasons why Lou is attempting to get his late grandfather the credit he feels he is deserving of. "I met the grandson in 1988," he recalls. "That was my last year at the monument."

The winners of the 2010 Ben Black Elk Award, named in honor of the Native American who greeted visitors to Mount Rushmore for 27 years, the Shaffs were key figures in the promotion of the South Dakota tourist industry.[118] The couple established Rushmore-Borglum Tours and began offering a variety of tour-related services at the monument and in the surrounding environs.[119]

They also played important roles in developing the state's Japanese marketing initiative called Friendship Japan, a visitor and business recruitment campaign run by the South Dakota Office of Tourism.[120]

Now a resident of Marco Island, Florida, Howard Shaff, 83, came across as a well-spoken, erudite man in a phone conversation he had with the author in September 2013. In principle, he admits, the Park Service "should give Del Bianco his due."

"My feeling is that, next to Borglum, nobody put more of their soul into the memorial than Del Bianco did," he continues. "Del Bianco was an extremely talented artist, but Borglum was the artist whom everybody listened to, everyone followed *his* instructions. He was responsible for the whole thing happening."

"I recognize what Del Bianco's grandson is trying to do, and there's a place for that," added Shaff. Nevertheless, he acknowledges not mentioning Luigi Del Bianco in his book either. "We were writing a book about Gutzon Borglum," stressed Shaff. "We weren't writing about the history of Mount Rushmore."

---

[118] www.sdvisit.com.
[119] Ibid.
[120] Ibid.

CHAPTER 6

ALL MEN MAY BE CREATED EQUAL, BUT...

According to Joint Resolution 175 of the 103rd Congress, Thomas Jefferson's famous phrase in the Declaration of Independence, "All men are created equal," was suggested by his friend, the Italian immigrant, physician and patriot Philip (Filippo) Mazzei.[121] No less than future United States President John F. Kennedy himself acknowledged this in his own book, *A Nation of Immigrants:*

> It was paraphrased from the writing of Philip Mazzei, an Italian-born patriot and pamphleteer, who was a close friend of Jefferson. A few alleged scholars try to discredit Mazzei as the creator of this statement and idea, saying that there is no mention of it anywhere until after the Declaration was published. This phrase appears in Italian in Mazzei's own hand, written in Italian, several years prior to the writing of the Declaration of Independence. Mazzei and Jefferson often exchanged ideas about true liberty and freedom. No one man can take complete credit for the ideals of American democracy.[122]

Writing under a pseudonym in the *Virginia Gazette* in 1774, Mazzei argued the following:

> Tutti gli uomini sono per natura egualmente liberi e indipendenti. Quest'eguaglianza è necessaria per costituire un governo libero. Bisogna che ognuno sia uguale all'altro nel diritto naturale.

---

[121] Congressional Record, Volume 140, Number 7, August 5, 1994.
[122] John F. Kennedy, *A Nation of Immigrants*, Anti-Defamation League, 1958.

All men are by nature equally free and independent. Such equality is necessary in order to create a free government. All men must be equal to each other in natural law.[123]

Great words, obviously. But they are *just* words. When men and women forget this important axiom, what happens? Prejudice and bigotry run free.

That seems almost unfathomable these days, especially when an African American was elected to occupy the White House, in 2008, and then re-elected four years later. But if there weren't any bigots still among us, we wouldn't need human rights commissions and tribunals, would we?

Hate crimes are not a thing of the past. They're just directed at new groups. Try convincing the lesbian, gay, bisexual, and transgender (LGBT) community in your neighborhood otherwise.

Or the Muslim community, for that matter. Or someone with acquired immunodeficiency syndrome (AIDS).

Lest we forget, it wasn't that many years ago that the trifecta of African Americans, Jewish Americans and, in particular, Italian Americans faced outright hatred. For their views. For their dress. For their traditions.

For just being blacks, Jews and Italians.

Hatred of Italians, in particular, has been in vogue for centuries. In the 16th Century, for instance, John Calvin, the reformer who helped establish the Reformist Church of Switzerland, described Italians as lazy, two-faced and deceitful. [124]

Further, in *Are Italians White? How Race is Made in America*, author Jennifer Guglielmo writes that the United States government's execution of Italian immigrants and anarchists Nicola Sacco and Bartolomeo Vanzetti, seven years after their highly inconclu-

---

[123] Librizziancestorsinmyheart.blogspot.com, July 3, 2010.
[124] Amir Seliman, "Immigration Atrocities in the Land of Opportunity; The Path of Social Justice," Rutgers University, 2011.

sive trial for the shooting of two men during a 1920 robbery, had the effect of stigmatizing Italian immigrants as outlaws and political subversives from there on.[125]

If ethnic stereotypes didn't exist, why would former United States Senator of Kentucky Jim Bunning, who was running for reelection in 2004, describe his opponent, Daniel Mongiardo, as "looking like one of Saddam Hussein's sons."?[126] He also referred to one of Mongiardo's supporters as "a thug."[127]

And, while serving in the Legislative Assembly of Ontario, career politician Ed Havrot in 1979 repeatedly interrupted a speech by another member, Tony Lupusella, by yelling, "This is the wop show."[128]

Small wonder, then, that Italian Americans have often tried to stay as under the radar as possible.

Take Domenico Nicolo, for example. Not the current Professor of Economics at the University of Reggio Calabria, but rather the Italian immigrant from Torricella Peligna, Italy buried in St. Ambrose Cemetery in Deadwood, South Dakota. According to FindAGrave.com, Domenico immigrated to America in 1902 to join his brother Berardino Nicolo, in Deadwood, where the promise of a better life in the States awaited him.[129]

While it is tempting to suggest that their lives in South Dakota were problem free, in order to enjoy their time in this country, do you know what they did? *They both changed their surnames.*

Meet the Roberts Brothers; Frank (Berardino) and Thomas (Domenico).[130]

Of course, without specific proof of any bigoted incidents they

---

[125] Jennifer Guglielmo, "White Lies, Dark Truths," *Are Italians White? How Race is Made in America,* Routledge, 2003.
[126] *USA Today*, April 1, 2004.
[127] Ibid.
[128] Eric Dowd, *The Ottawa Journal*, November 1, 1979.
[129] www.findagrave.com.
[130] Ibid.

may have experienced or been subjected to, it's impossible to know what motivated them to do what they did. But it stands to reason that proud Italian immigrants to this country — on their headstones, both Domenico and his wife, Maria's, Italian names are used[131] — would not have felt compelled to change their names if society was totally approving of them.

When it comes to societal attitudes about immigrants, the federal government hasn't always helped matters, either. Since representatives and senators always have to be attuned to the whims of their constituents, in 1921 Congress passed legislation limiting the number of immigrants from one country to three percent of that country's foreign-born total already in the United States as of the 1910 Census.[132]

Three years later, Congress toughened things for foreigners even more; the Johnson-Reed Immigration Act of 1924 limited the number of immigrants from one country to two percent of that country's foreign born total already in the States as of the 1890 Census.[133]

There are plenty of cases over the years of xenophobia run amok. For instance, in his *An Immigrant Heritage: South Dakota's Foreign-Born in the Era of Assimilation,* Rex C. Myers writes that, amid the anti-German backlash resulting from World War I, South Dakota's Council of Defense on February 25, 1918 issued a letter to all educational institutions proclaiming that the teaching of the German language in public schools, college, universities and other institutions of learning within South Dakota was detrimental to the best interests of the nation.[134] Three months later, the council banned the German language entirely.[135] This prohibition extended

---

[131] Ibid.
[132] Myers, *An Immigrant Heritage: South Dakota's Foreign Born in the Era of Assimilation,* South Dakota State Historical Society, 1989.
[133] Ibid.
[134] Ibid.
[135] Ibid.

to church services and reached the point at which all churches in the German-Russian community of Eureka, South Dakota were closed and locked by school authorities, explains Myers.[136] Cities such as Yankton and Faulkton, Myers adds, even had burnings of German books.[137]

With respect to the Italian experience in America, perhaps the most famous incident of malevolent behavior was the lynching of 11 Italian-Americans in New Orleans in 1891.

In an online article for Cable News Network in July 2012, acclaimed Italian author Ed Falco, who penned the novel *The Family Corleone*, writes that the March 14, 1891 incident was the largest mass lynching in U.S. history.[138] After nine Italians were tried and found not guilty of murdering New Orleans Police Chief David Hennessy, explains Falco, a mob dragged them from the jail, along with two other Italians who were being held on unrelated charges, and lynched them all.[139] The lynchings, he continues, were followed by mass arrests of Italian immigrants throughout New Orleans and waves of attacks against Italians nationwide.[140]

In a March 16, 1891 editorial, that venerable paper of record, *The New York Times,* referred to the Italians as "sneaking and cowardly Sicilians, the descendants of bandits and assassins."

Mind you, these were the men who had just been *exonerated* in a court of law and who were to be released the very next morning.

The New Orleans Democrat was especially instrumental in working people up — the paper reported that "the little jail was crowded with Sicilians, whose low, receding foreheads, dark skin, repulsive countenances and slovenly attire proclaimed their brutal nature."[141]

No less than future United States President Theodore Roosevelt

---

[136] Ibid.
[137] Ibid.
[138] Ed Falco, "When Italian Immigrants Were the Other," CNN.com, July 10, 2012.
[139] Ibid.
[140] Ibid.
[141] David Pacchioli, "Dark Legacy," *Penn State News,* May 1, 2004.

called the lynchings "a rather good thing."[142]

In *A People's History of the United States*, the late Howard Zinn (a political science professor at the author's alma mater) wrote that Roosevelt was contemptuous of races and nations he considered inferior.[143] About the lynchings, notes Zinn, Roosevelt privately told his sister in a letter that he acknowledged "saying as much (that the lynchings were a good thing) at a dinner with 'various dago diplomats ... all wrought up by the lynching.'"[144]

Actor Arch Elwein who, like Lou Del Bianco, is a fixture at grade school assemblies, usually performing in South Dakota, North Dakota and Montana, plays Roosevelt in one of the various programs he does. Elwein, for one, believes that Zinn took Roosevelt's comments out of context. "I believe TR's statement to his sister has more to do with vigilantism than Italians," he wrote in an email to the author.[145]

When asked about his famous relative's anti-Italianism, Kermit "Kim" Roosevelt III, TR's great-great-grandson who is a law professor at the University of Pennsylvania, where he specializes in both conflicts of law and constitutional law, told the author in an email that "every revered figure of our history said, did or believed things that are reprehensible by modern standards.[146]

"George Washington owned slaves. Abraham Lincoln talked of blacks as inferior,"[147] continued Roosevelt, who once clerked for former United States Supreme Court Justice David Souter. A novelist who authored the 2005 legal thriller, *In the Shadow of the Law*, Roosevelt added that, "we understand such people much better by

---

[142] Richard Gambino, *Blood of My Blood; The Dilemma of the Italian Americans*, Doubleday & Company, 1974.
[143] Howard Zinn, *A People's History of the United States*, Harper Perennial Modern Classics, 2005.
[144] Ibid.
[145] In an August 28, 2013 email to the author.
[146] In an August 26, 2013 email to the author.
[147] Ibid.

focusing on the ways that they challenged the prejudices of their time, rather than the ways they reflected them."[148] As an example, he pointed out how TR once invited Booker T. Washington to dine at the White House with him in 1901.[149]

"(That) shocked much of the country and triggered unprecedented attacks on him but shifted the national conversation on race," he concluded.[150]

While it is true that times and attitudes have changed, it still seems more than ironic that Roosevelt's sculpted face on the monument was shaped, in part, by one of these "dagos."

"America has a proud tradition as an immigrant nation," wrote Falco, who is a professor of English at Virginia Tech, where he leads the Masters of Fine Arts Program in Creative Writing. "But it also has a long history of marginalizing those it marks as 'other.'"[151]

Again, the role of the press in perpetuating this idea cannot be overstated. For instance, in July 1892, Thomas Bailey Aldrich published a poem in *Atlantic Monthly* that began as follows — "Wide open and unguarded stand our gates, and then through them passes a wild motley throng."[152]

Not exactly Emma Lazarus' "Give me your tired, your poor, your huddled masses yearning to be free,"[153] is it?

The "other" concept was also broached by writer Justin Demetri in a 2009 essay. In *Italians in America: From Discrimination to Adoration*, Demetri argued that part of the reason Italian immigrants to this country were treated so badly was that they were seen as unintelligent, menial laborers.[154] "They were willing to work in de-

---

[148] Ibid.
[149] Ibid.
[150] Ibid.
[151] Falco, "When Italian Immigrants Were the Other," CNN.com, July 10, 2012.
[152] Thomas Bailey Aldrich, "Unguarded Gates," *Atlantic Monthly*, 1892.
[153] Emma Lazarus, "The New Colossus," 1883.
[154] Justin Demetri, "Italians in America; From Discrimination to Adoration," www.lifeinitaly.com, 2009.

plorable conditions, especially on first arrival," explained Demetri.[155]

"Many of the first Italian fishermen of Gloucester, Massachusetts settled there after years of doing nearly anything from working in rail yards and stables to mining for gold in California," he added.[156] "The determination of these first immigrants to support their families was apparently misunderstood as a slave or servant mentality. It is a theme that is still current today in America — the native residents accused the immigrants of taking their jobs, underselling them by working longer hours for much lower wages.

"What observers at the time did not realize was that these industrious men and women were just starting out on the ground floor," continued Demetri.[157] "This backbreaking and often degrading labor was just a stepping stone to acceptance and legitimacy within American society. The first generation suffered to make life easier for the generations to come."[158]

Against this backdrop, it is certainly not hard to imagine that, when Del Bianco arrived in South Dakota, he was seen as the quintessential outsider.

✳ ✳ ✳

In an email to the author, the Pennington County Sherriff's Office indicated that their records for acts of prejudice "in the Keystone area at the time of the carving of Mount Rushmore do not date back" to the 1930s.[159]

Nonetheless, with respect to bias and bigotry, South Dakota has somewhat of a checkered past. For instance, according to the Southern Poverty Law Center, in December 2003 a swastika and a Celtic cross was spray-painted on the front door of a Jewish temple

---

[155] Ibid.
[156] Ibid.
[157] Ibid.
[158] Ibid.
[159] In a September 17, 2013 email to the author.

in Sioux Falls.[160] Six years later, in March 2009, four white teens and one adolescent fired a BB gun and threw urine at Native Americans in Rapid City.[161]

African Americans in South Dakota weren't immune from prejudice either.

On December 11, 1962, the South Dakota Advisory Committee to the United States Civil Rights Commission held a public meeting to investigate discrimination involving the African-American airmen who were assigned to the Ellsworth Air Force Base in Rapid City.[162]

Of the 4,320 enlisted men and 673 officers assigned at the base, 354 of the enlisted men and five of the officers were African Americans.[163] President Harry S. Truman had issued an Executive Order barring discrimination in the Armed Forces in 1948.

So when complaints of discrimination in off-base housing and the unavailability of public accommodations found their way to the Commission, an advisory committee was formed to investigate the allegations.

In its March 1963 report, the Commission included testimony from hundreds of people, both Caucasian and African-American, regarding the tenor of racial relations in Rapid City. What did the report conclude? Things weren't all warm and fuzzy in Rapid City.

"The evidence gathered by the South Dakota Advisory Committee to the United States Commission on Civil Rights provides the basis for the unqualified conclusion that Negro airmen stationed at Ellsworth Air Force Base, and their families, experience discrimination in Rapid City to the extent that it is, in the Presi-

---

[160] Southern Poverty Law Center.
[161] Ibid.
[162] "Negro Airmen in a Northern Community; Discrimination in Rapid City, South Dakota: A Report of the South Dakota Advisory Committee to the United States Commission on Civil Rights," March 1963, Thurgood Marshall Law Library, University of Maryland School of Law.
[163] Ibid.

dent's words, 'a serious source of hardship and embarrassment,'" the report noted.[164]

Here's a June 2, 1961 editorial from the *Rapid City Journal* that the report referenced:[165]

> The problem of coping with Negroes is not new, but has never been solved for Rapid City because of several unfortunate occurrences. There were bars in Rapid City which served Negroes until "gangs" of Negroes were "taking over" the places ... the actions of a minority of the Negroes in this area have impaired progress for integration ... the problem for Rapid City is apparent and if the malcontents who are moved to Ellsworth Air Force Base would resolve to behave themselves as law-abiding citizens, some progress could be made.

Mind you, these "malcontents" were defending the liberties and freedoms — such as freedom of the press — that the folks who ran the newspaper obviously enjoyed. But the editorialists took the 'blame the victim' tact, rather than blame the Caucasian business owners who were no doubt the real individuals at fault.

Fifteen years later, enlightenment still seemingly escaped certain people living in South Dakota. In the foreword to her 2007 memoir *Hapa Girl*, author May-Lee Chai describes the reaction she and her family engendered when they first moved to Vermillion after her father, an academician named Winberg, accepted a vice-presidency at the University of South Dakota:[166]

> We would stop traffic just by walking down the sidewalk.... I didn't know then, when I was twelve, that they were staring because they'd never seen a Chinese man with a white woman be-

---

[164] Ibid.
[165] Ibid.
[166] May-lee Chai, *Hapa Girl: A Memoir*, Temple University Press, 2007.

fore, and a blonde woman at that. I didn't know they thought we were brazen, flaunting our family in public. It was 1979, and we had imagined that the segregated past was just that, past.

In its review of Chai's book, the *Christian Science Monitor* noted that, "the Chai family is anything but welcome in the xenophobic town, historically infused with anti-native American hatred and violence ... with nowhere to go, they remain trapped in the suffocating town." [167]

Chai writes that, due to the bad economy in Vermillion, the locals were probably envious of her father, so they took their frustration and anger over their own situations out on him:

It felt as though we were being published for crimes we hadn't realized we had committed.... There were many people who wanted my father to suffer. They were going to show this "Chinaman" his place.[168]

The locals were so hardened against this "outsider" that the Chai family house was shot at from passing cars and their pet dogs were gunned down on their own lawn.[169]

Given this sort of narrow-minded, parochial attitude, should anyone really be surprised that they don't celebrate Columbus Day in South Dakota?

In 2009, Frank J. Cavaioli, Professor Emeritus at the State University of New York at Farmingdale, wrote a column for the *Florida Sun Sentinel* pointing out that, in 1992, "at the time of the quincentennial celebration of the discovery of America, revisionist historians had charged Columbus with causing slavery, ecocide, dis-

---

[167] Terry Hong, "Growing Up a Hapa Girl in America," *The Christian Science Monitor*, May 1, 2007.
[168] Chai, *Hapa Girl: A Memoir*, Temple University Press, 2007.
[169] Hong, Growing Up a Hapa Girl in America," *The Christian Science Monitor*, May 1, 2007.

ease and destruction of native populations in the New World.[170]

"Columbus-bashing may be considered a more subtle version of anti-Italian-American prejudice, though many will not admit it," he wrote.[171]

Why doesn't South Dakota celebrate Columbus Day? Perhaps because of the amount of Native Americans who reside in the state, South Dakota celebrates the second Monday in October as an official state holiday known as Native American Day rather than Columbus Day.

While the failure of the South Dakota Legislature and its leaders not to commemorate Columbus Day isn't conclusive proof of anything, it is curious, nonetheless. Only Hawaii, Alaska and South Dakota don't recognize the holiday.

As for Del Bianco, although there is no firsthand proof that he encountered any sort of prejudice while working and living in Keystone, particularly since he didn't talk much about his experiences at Mount Rushmore, one letter from no less than Borglum himself is very revealing.

In his June 1933 correspondence to Boland, of the Mount Rushmore National Memorial Commission, Borglum bemoans the fact that there is a dearth of seasoned, well-trained men working under him.[172] He then goes on to note that:

> I notified ... my son, Lincoln, who was here pointing, that I was bringing with me an assistant, a semi-sculptor who had been with me off and on in the east for twelve years, a powerful, capable granite man, whom I had converted into an efficient marble cutter. I was immediately notified that his presence here was objected to and that the Rapid City office did not want him. I ignored this and put him immediately in charge of the work....

---

[170] Frank J. Cavaioli, "On Columbus Day, Celebrate Our History," *Florida Sun Sentinel*, October 11, 2009.

[171] Ibid.

[172] Gutzon Borglum Papers, Manuscript Division, Library of Congress, Washington, D.C.

He complained to me within a week of the treatment he was being accorded from the Rapid City office, including rudeness, insolence and petty dickering about wages.[173]

Why was Del Bianco's presence objected to? Why wasn't he wanted? These are all questions that may never be answered. But we can still ponder over them.

Of course, prejudice can be blatant or benign, overt or subtle. Even the most popular Italian American of his time, the gifted DiMaggio, wasn't immune from subtle prejudice. In an article for *Life Magazine*, author Noel Busch wrote that, "although Joe learned Italian first, Joe ... speaks English without an accent and is otherwise well adapted to most United States mores. Instead of olive oil or smelly grease, he keeps his hair slick with water. He never reeks of garlic and prefers chicken chow mein to spaghetti."[174]

Mind you, there doesn't always have to be subtle or benign bigotry at work. Sometimes the prejudice is openly hostile. In an essay for *American Speech Magazine*, John M. Lipski of Michigan State University writes that deliberate mispronunciation of foreign names stems from a general desire to belittle or ridicule members of minority ethnic groups.[175] "Consider, for example, the pronunciation of *Italian* as *Eye-talian*," observes Lipski. "Individuals who use the latter pronunciation generally do so consistently [and] it is significant that this variant is frequently found among those with a low regard for Italians."[176]

Further, in 1923, psychologist Carl C. Brigham, using the results of Intelligence Quotient (IQ) tests, concluded that 83% of Jews, 80% of Hungarians, and 70% of Italians were feeble minded and

---

[173] Ibid.
[174] Noel Busch, "Joe DiMaggio," *Life*, April 30, 1939.
[175] John M. Lipski, "Prejudice and Pronunciation," *American Speech Magazine*, The American Dialect Society, Vol. 51, Spring-Summer 1976.
[176] Ibid.

should consequently be excluded from citizenship in the United States.[177]

In Dr. Kristin J. Anderson's masterful *Benign Bigotry; The Psychology of Subtle Prejudice*, the University of Houston professor explains that we are all apt to make judgments about behavioral tendencies and personalities if we think that people who all look alike also all act alike.[178]

Why does this happen, she asks? Construing people as out group members —those who look alike and act alike — provides a sense of predictability.[179] According to Dr. Anderson, people in the dominant group can be more selective in their social contacts and might not have a lot of contact with members of out groups because we have more information about in group members — those in the dominant group.[180] Therefore, the out-group members become stereotyped because no one needs to or wants to have detailed or accurate information about them.[181]

Of course, the group definition of who you are implies a definition of who you are not. The circle that includes "us" (the in group) excludes "them" (the out group). So for purposes of illustrating this concept, let's say that you're a miner in Keystone, South Dakota in the 1930s who has been hired to work at Mount Rushmore. Who's the out-group member? You or Luigi Del Bianco?

This is what many sociologists, psychologists and other chroniclers of human behavior call a "self-serving bias."[182] The Keystone miners more than likely felt comfortable with one another and distance from Del Bianco, who they knew nothing about. They there-

---

[177] Carl C. Brigham, *A Study in American Intelligence*, Princeton University Press, 1923.
[178] Kristin J. Anderson, *Benign Bigotry; The Psychology of Subtle Prejudice*, Cambridge University Press, 2010.
[179] Ibid.
[180] Ibid.
[181] Ibid.
[182] Hart Blanton, Jennifer Crocker and Dale Miller, "The Effects of In-Group versus Out-Group Social Comparison on Self-Esteem in the Context of a Negative Stereotype," *Journal of Experimental Social Psychology*, Volume 36, 2000.

fore felt better about themselves.

But did that necessarily make them bigots or prejudiced people?

While South Dakota's people have often gotten a bad rap over the years because of some highly publicized incidents, it is important to remember there are good people and bad apples everywhere. The author of *Searching for Italy in America's Rural Heartland*, Celeste Calvitto, who resided in South Dakota from 2002-2009, acknowledged that in an email to the author. "I never felt like an outsider in South Dakota, even with an Italian name," she wrote.[183]

Calvitto, who interviewed people in rural areas of six states for her book, added that most of the folks she talked to "said they didn't encounter any issues. Some speculated that the lack of prejudice had to do with the communities they settled in, which had immigrants from many nations.[184]

"There are a number of families of Italian descent that I know of who have been in western South Dakota for generations, and no one mentioned any sort of prejudice," she continued. "But of course, that doesn't mean it didn't occur. It just never came up in our conversations."[185]

---

[183] In a September 5, 2013 email to the author.
[184] Ibid.
[185] Ibid.

Luigi Del Bianco in Gutzon Borglum's studio at Mount Rushmore with the models for George Washington and Abraham Lincoln. Notice the torso and full dress on Washington; Borglum had originally planned to make Rushmore more than just the four faces, but lack of funding, skilled laborers and faulty rock precluded that.

Luigi's three sons, circa 1935: from left are Silvio, Caesar and Lou's late father, Vincent Del Bianco.

Lou Del Bianco with the marble bust his late grandfather, Luigi, carved of himself in 1921 -- when he was 29-years-old. (Photo courtesy of Jananne Abel, Westmore News)

CHAPTER 7

"UNREWARDED GENIUS IS ALMOST A PROVERB"

Not surprisingly, Wikipedia, the free online encyclopedia used as a research tool by scholars and students alike, has a page dealing with the construction of Mount Rushmore.

It should also come as no surprise that this page doesn't mention Luigi Del Bianco at all.

Instead, Ivan Houser, whom Lincoln Borglum replaced as assistant sculptor when the former left the project to pursue his own artistic ambitions, is the person who receives a prominent mention.

Houser, who taught ceramics and industrial design for 16 years, from 1950 to 1966 at Lewis & Clark College, in Portland, Oregon,[186] was the father of John Sherrill Houser, who eclipsed his own relative's accomplishments as a sculptor. One of his works, *The Equestrian,* took ten years to make and stands more than four stories tall and weighs in at 34,000 pounds. Located at the entrance of the El Paso (Texas) International Airport, it is the world's largest equestrian bronze statue.[187]

More recently, John Sherrill Houser created a bronze bust of Nobel Prize-winning scientist Francis Crick that was unveiled at the University of Cambridge on July 7, 2012.[188]

Born in South Dakota, John Sherrill Houser grew up around a man who some might argue was even more valuable to Gutzon Borglum at Mount Rushmore than Luigi Del Bianco.

---

[186] Archives and Special Collections, Lewis & Clark College.
[187] www.visitelpaso.com.
[188] Francis Crick Memorial Conference Newsletter, University of Cambridge, Edition 1, May 23, 2012.

John Sherrill Houser has never attempted to trumpet Ivan Houser's contributions to Mount Rushmore in the same manner as Lou has been doing with respect to Luigi. But that doesn't mean he doesn't think his late father isn't deserving of more recognition either.

"I thought he'd get more credit," says the 77-year-old sculptor during a telephone interview. "I thought a lot of people should get more credit, not just my dad, but Luigi and Bill Tallman too."

"The artistic endowment and high abilities of Luigi del Bianco, as Borglum's chief carver, were significant factors in Mount Rushmore's development and public recognition of his contribution is long overdue," wrote Houser in a follow-up email to the author.[189]

According to John Houser, his father was fresh from the Art Students League in New York City when he met Borglum during the Great Depression. Times being what they were, Ivan Houser was quickly hired to do work on the mountain.[190]

Initially, says Houser, Ivan was hired to hang over the granite faces in a bosun's chair and mark points for the carving to come — at 45 cents an hour.[191] Later, however, as assistant sculptor he did much of the sculpting on the enlarging models developed from Borglum's first maquette.[192] "These intermediate heads can still be viewed in the historic Sculptor's Studio on site," he added.[193]

At the close of each workday, explains Houser, Ivan and the chief enlarger, William Tallman, took measurements from these models; the measurements were then sent to Luigi and the men at the top of the monument who removed the stone.[194] "But this was not a mere mechanical task," Sherrill Houser noted. "One of Del Bianco's responsibilities was to supervise and ensure the sculptural

---

[189] In an October 21, 2013 email to the author.
[190] Ibid.
[191] Ibid.
[192] Ibid.
[193] Ibid.
[194] Ibid.

integrity and accuracy of this colossal work as it progressed.

"Too often in glorifying the accomplishment of a 'great individual' like Borglum, we are blinded to the supportive contributions of others who were equally indispensable in its realization," added Houser. "As a monumental sculptor myself, I am very aware of the communal dedication required to achieve such a project."[195]

Which begets the logical questions: What is the mindset of an artist? What does he or she have a right to expect when it comes to a finished work of art? And should anyone have even expected Gutzon Borglum to publicly extol Luigi's contributions in the first place?

To help answer those questions, the author asked someone who would know — the acclaimed South Dakota sculptor John Lopez, whose bronze statues of various United States Presidents can be seen lining the streets of Rapid City, as part of The City of Presidents Project that was started 14 years ago.[196] Part of the Rapid City Historic District Tour, the series of life-size bronze statues of our nation's past presidents are featured all along the city's streets and sidewalks.[197]

A graduate of Northern State University, in Aberdeen, South Dakota, Lopez grew up on a ranch, so his early pieces reflected the things he knew best; horses, cows, cowboys and prairie wildlife. In 2000, the Pro Rodeo Hall of Fame commissioned him to create two bronze monuments for their sculpture garden. The first featured World Champion Calf Roper Paul Tierney on a horse named Coffee Jeff; the second monument featured eleven-time world champion barrel racer Charmayne James on her horse, Scamper.[198]

Based in Lemmon, South Dakota, Lopez — who recently started experimenting in scrap iron metal sculpturing — acknowledged

---

[195] Ibid.
[196] www.visitrapidcity.com.
[197] Ibid.
[198] www.lopez-ranch.net.

that he was initially not familiar with Luigi's role in the creation of Mount Rushmore. However, after doing some research of his own, he admitted that it was clear that Luigi "played a very pivotal role in the carving of the mountain.[199]

"As his association with Borglum predated Mount Rushmore, it is clear that Borglum came into the project trusting him and depending on him," Lopez continued. "It was Del Bianco who did the subtle carving to give the faces expression and life. It was he who carved the life into Lincoln's eyes … his value to the project is indisputable."[200]

However, while Lopez conceded he was disappointed that the Del Bianco name is not more well known than it is, it didn't surprise him, either.

"When I was a sculptor's assistant, I did what my mentor asked of me, without expecting to share in the fame," recalls Lopez. "I was honored to be given the chance to learn from another's experience and to take part in some amazing projects. Then when I was able to establish my own studio, I applied those skills I learned from my teacher. In turn, I have had the chance to mentor some aspiring artists.[201]

"Well known artists worked with apprentices, and some masterpieces attributed to a master may well be the work of an apprentice, or significantly influenced by an apprentice," continued Lopez. "So it is not unusual that Del Bianco was not given credit. Unrewarded genius is almost a proverb."[202]

Lopez then made an interesting observation: though Luigi may have been, as Borglum described him, a "powerful, capable granite man" whom he "had converted into an efficient marble cutter," the fact that he didn't go on to create significant art of his own might

---

[199] In an October 18, 2013 email to the author.
[200] Ibid.
[201] Ibid.
[202] Ibid.

be the reason very few people know of him.[203]

It would be hard to dispute Lopez's point of view. In his post-Mount Rushmore life, Del Bianco returned to Port Chester and operated a stone cutting business from his studio on Clinton Street, where he carved about 500 gravestones in St. Mary's Cemetery from rough Vermont marble. He also was responsible for the fine statuary at the Corpus Christi Church, the Lady of Fatima statute at the Holy Rosary School and the Spanish-American War Memorial in the town's Summerfield Park.

That kind of work put food on the table to feed his family, and was clearly appreciated. But he certainly never did work approaching the level that he had done with Borglum on the Wars of America Memorial, in Newark, New Jersey.

To say nothing of the work he did in the Black Hills of South Dakota.

"The fact that he did not go on to create significant art of his own, though he had the skills and the experience, may signal that he was not, at heart, an 'artist'," suggested Lopez. "Perhaps he was a very skilled craftsman, but he lacked artistic genius."[204]

Of Lou's efforts to get Luigi the recognition he feels he has gone far too long without, Lopez is sympathetic, if also somewhat guarded. "While the name of the head carver of Mount Rushmore may never become a household name, that does not mean that all efforts to alleviate the situation should not be taken," he concluded.[205]

---

[203] Ibid.
[204] Ibid.
[205] Ibid.

Luigi (left) and Primo Carnera, who won the heavyweight boxing championship at Madison Square Garden on June 27, 1933. Carnera was from a neighboring village in the Italian Province of Pordenone.

CHAPTER 8

IN DEFENSE OF "DADDY"

In Los Angeles, California one morning in late September 2013, a 67-year-old woman who works for an Internet marketing company takes time out of her day to talk with justifiable pride about her father.

"Of course, I always heard things about what he did," says Gloria Del Bianco, of Luigi's work. "But I never understood the magnitude of them."

"I mean, I was raised by this man, who I always thought was the end all and be all anyway," she continues. "So growing up I thought all the things I heard about his work at the monument from my brothers and mother was just perfectly natural."

"Caesar used to make fun of me all the time," she adds. "He used to joke, 'Oh, well you weren't even a thought back then,'" recalls Gloria, who was born in 1946.

No longer in her salad days, Gloria these days does think a lot about what she calls her father's rightful place in history. Angry that Luigi isn't getting the credit her family feels he is deserving of, she says she is adamant that the Park Service address this slight.

"I'm not ready yet to say it's a slap in the face yet," she maintains. "But I'm pretty close to that."

More than anything, Gloria cannot understand how, in spite of being made aware of all of Gutzon Borglum's own paperwork, the Park Service continues to lump Luigi in with the likes of, say, a Clifford or Edwald Hayes.

"How can they turn a blind eye to all that documentation that Caesar and Lou found?," she asks. "I just don't understand it."

Neither does family friend Jim Sapione who, along with his wife, Judy, accompanied Lou and Caesar on one of their trips to the Library of Congress and the National Archives to comb through Borglum's papers.

"I could understand the government's attitude if there wasn't any documentation," says the 77-year-old Sapione, who was working as the facilities manager at the Albert Einstein College of Medicine when, due to a property management conference he had to attend in Washington, D.C., he volunteered to go on one of Lou and Caesar's road trips. "It'd just be about a family member's pride in their relative. But there's all that paperwork, it just doesn't add up."

"It's incongruous to me why the government isn't doing right by Luigi," continues Sapione who, when he served as the supervisor for the Town of Rye, New York, says he instructed Caesar to contact then United States Senator Alfonse D'Amato of New York for assistance.

"I figured D'Amato was a fellow Italian, and he'd be able to exert the sort of political pressure to get the government to do something," explains Sapione, who now resides in Virginia. "But Caesar didn't want to try that."

"Not to speak ill of the dead, but Caesar was often an unrealistic person, and really, really naive," continues Sapione, who remembers that he had to vouch for Caesar's identity when the two arrived at the Library of Congress.

"He didn't drive a car, so he didn't have any driver's license to present to the officials there," recalls Sapione with a laugh. "He didn't use any credit cards, either; Caesar actually thought he was going to enter that building just by telling the guards that he was the son of the chief carver of Mount Rushmore."

According to Sapione, Caesar said he trusted the Mount Rushmore official he was in contact with at the time and that he was confident the man would do right by his father. "I felt this man was just bullshitting Caesar and yessing him to death and stringing him along and jerking him around," adds Sapione, who says he's also counseled Lou not to be too much of a diplomatist when dealing with the federal government.

That man who Caesar had confidence in would have been the then Superintendent of Mount Rushmore, Daniel Wenk, who is now in charge of Yellowstone National Park.[206] Wenk was superintendent at the monument from 1985 to 2001 and, according to a Park Service press release, his leadership was integral in raising $60 million in private funds for the monument — presumably in concert with the Mount Rushmore Society.[207]

Contacted by email in October 2013, Wenk confirmed the agency's party line.

"It was the position of the National Park Service not to call attention, or honor any particular worker at the Memorial," he told the author.[208] "During the time of the redesign of the facilities at the Memorial a great deal of discussion and debate occurred over the idea to place a bust of the sculptor Gutzon Borglum in the main visitor area. It was ultimately determined that it was appropriate for him to be recognized, along with the workers, in an area designated as Borglum Court along the main walkway leading to the Memorial viewing areas."[209]

"No individual recognition was considered beyond that during my tenure," continued Wenk. "The purpose of the Memorial was to honor the contributions of the four presidents to our nation's birth, growth, preservation, and expansion."[210]

In 1995, Gloria's curiosity prompted her to contact Mount Rushmore directly. The official whom she spoke to was James G. Popovich, the then Chief of Interpretation Services: "So I called him up and said, 'You've got all this correspondence, all these let-

---

[206] National Park Service, October 5, 2010
[207] Ibid.
[208] In an October 17, 2013 email to the author.
[209] Ibid.
[210] Ibid.

ters from Borglum himself, and you're not doing a damn thing,' she says she told Popovich. 'What's the problem here? What's the issue?' she continues. 'And he told me the same thing that Lou has been up against, the same party line, that 'This is just the way we see it, your father was just a worker here'.'"

That's when Gloria says she forgot her manners and erupted.

"He was brusque and curt and rude to me," she says of Popovich. "So I finally snapped and told him, 'I'm gonna sue you sons of bitches!'"

Popovich, who retired from the agency in 2004, famously nixed the idea of adding the face of President Ronald Reagan to the monument when it was floated by United States Representative Matt Salmon of Arizona in 1999.[211]

"Lincoln Borglum, when he left the project in 1941, said there wasn't any other carvable granite on Mount Rushmore to do any other figures," Popovich told the *Associated Press*. "And we pretty much believe that to be true."[212]

In retrospect, Gloria acknowledges that taking the federal government to court over her father's work at Mount Rushmore wasn't one of the smartest things to ever come out of her mouth. "I said it in the heat of the moment," she admits.

"But I'm still mad," she adds. "And I'm disappointed Lou has to deal with the same bullshit."

✳ ✳ ✳

Twelve hundred miles away from Los Angeles, in Lincoln, Nebraska, another woman who is proud of her father is asked about the monument. But Rex Allen Smith's daughter, Mary Charney Smith Nelson, is being contacted for an entirely different reason.

A soft-spoken woman who is a regular churchgoer and trained musician, Smith Nelson is the principal oboist for the Hastings

---

[211] "The New Face of Mount Rushmore," *Associated Press*, January 30, 1999.
[212] Ibid.

Symphony Orchestra (HSO); she has performed with the Lincoln and Omaha Symphonies, as well.

"Orchestras are families," she told the *Prairie Fire*, of Lincoln, "and HSO is a family that gets along most of the time."[213]

Members of her extended family, however, are a different story. Her stepsister, Cindy Luterman, of Texas, refused to respond to the author's repeated requests for an interview (her husband, Ed, said that Smith "just married Cindy's mother. We really don't have anything to do with his family").

Smith Nelson, on the other hand, was as gracious as could be to a total stranger who she visited with on the telephone in August 2013. Her cooperative nature and agreeableness to answer the author's questions about her late father's failure to mention Del Bianco in his book was even more impressive considering how awkward the subject matter must have been for her.

"I hope you realize I'm not upset at all that you'd wonder why my dad left Mr. Del Bianco out of his book," she wrote the author in a followup email afterwards. "If I were you I would have wondered, too."[214]

There are any number of reasons why Smith might have left Del Bianco out of his book. For starters, since Luigi passed away in 1969, he wasn't around to be interviewed by Smith, whose book was published by Abbeville Press in 1994.

But since Villa, who died in 1948, *was* included in the book, that explanation doesn't hold much water.

Perhaps Smith didn't have any contact information for a Del Bianco relative? Lou himself debunks that theory.

"I personally attempted to call Mr. Smith on several occasions," he says. "He just never called me back.

"I've always felt that Smith wanted to emphasize the unem-

---

[213] Liz Case, "Hastings Symphony Soon to Celebrate 90th Consecutive Season," *Prairie Fire*, August 2013.
[214] In an August 31, 2013 email to the author.

ployed miners so much in his book that, if he introduced my grandfather into the story, that wouldn't be good for the tale he was telling," explains Lou. "Borglum brought in Luigi, this professional stone carver, this ringer, and if Smith wrote about him, that would just detract away from the miners getting the credit he felt they were deserving of."

Smith Nelson agrees that her father wanted the Keystone miners to be in the spotlight.

"Daddy was pretty excited about interviewing the miners who'd done the actual carving," she continued. "From the way he talked about it, it sounded to me like he believed that nobody else had ever been interested in finding out the carvers' stories and writing them up. Daddy thought interviewing them was his fortuitous brainwave, that he was doing something new and significant, something different and real and worthwhile."[215]

"He didn't want his book to be another hymn to Gutzon Borglum," Smith Nelson added. "He wanted to show that, as with any enterprise of this size, the carving of Mount Rushmore was a group effort. He said over and over that he wanted to make his book be not just about the process but about the people who made it all happen."[216]

As for why Del Bianco was left out of *The Carving of Mount Rushmore*, Smith Nelson says that the simplest reason was that her father "just didn't know about him."[217]

In fact, Smith Nelson maintained that, if her father had actually known that an Italian immigrant to these shores was the chief carver at Mount Rushmore, he would have gone out of his way to include that salient fact in the book. "Dad loved learning about other cultures and other peoples," she said.[218]

---

[215] Ibid.
[216] Ibid.
[217] Ibid.
[218] Ibid.

"The idea that my dad would leave Mr. Del Bianco out because he was Italian ... is just nuts," she wrote.[219]

Mark Vargo, the State's Attorney for Pennington County, agrees with Smith Nelson. "It doesn't matter what kind of American carved the Mountain,"[220] he told the author via email. The grandson of immigrants from Eastern Europe, Vargo — who acknowledged that he heretofore didn't know the ethnicity of the monument's chief carver — nonetheless maintained that "the strength of this country is its ability to incorporate the best of all of us.[221]

"Mt. Rushmore, to me, stands for the cultural and political unity which the United States, at its best, represents," he continued. "That is what I see in the Mountain."[222]

South Dakota State Representative Mike Verchio agrees with Vargo and Smith Nelson. "I (also) doubt that his ethnicity had any impact on the situation," he told the author via email.[223]

A retired businessman who represents parts of Custer, Fall River and Pennington Counties in the South Dakota State Legislature,[224] Verchio — who is an Italian-American — admitted he was not aware of the fact that, with the exception of Gutzon and Lincoln Borglum, the Park Service classified all the individuals who worked at Mount Rushmore as one group, and that Del Bianco was not credited as the chief carver.[225]

"I would guess that Luigi was not the only person to work on the mountain who received minimal recognition for his contributions," continued Verchio, who serves on the South Dakota Legislature's Agriculture & Natural Resources Committee and who chairs

---

[219] Ibid.
[220] In a November 12, 2013 email to the author.
[221] Ibid.
[222] Ibid.
[223] In a October 25, 2013 email to the author.
[224] www.legis.sd.gov.
[225] In an October 25, 2013 email to the author.

its Transportation Committee.[226] A native of Iowa who is a former chamber of commerce executive,[227] Verchio agreed that, although the work Luigi did at the monument was a testament to "the amazing contributions" all ethnic groups that came to this country have made, he didn't see any point in introducing any specific resolution or proclamation commemorating Del Bianco, either.[228]

"No," he added. "Commemorations are a waste of taxpayers' money."[229]

Which is interesting since, during the Legislature's 2011 Session, Verchio signed on as a co-sponsor of House Commemoration #1002, which honored and supported Czech Days in Tabor, South Dakota.[230] That commemoration, in part, read as follows:

> Whereas, South Dakota's Czech immigrants have enriched our state's culture with their exceptional attainments in music, literature, and art, and are known for their love of agriculture, mechanical arts and democracy, which they strive to preserve for future generations;
>
> Now, therefore, be it commemorated, by the Eighty-sixth Legislature of the State of South Dakota, that the Legislature congratulates all South Dakotans of Czech ancestry and invites everyone to participate in the sixty-third annual Czech days on June 16, 17 and 18, 2011.[231]

A Republican who has a flawless attendance record, Verchio says on his campaign website that he doesn't "have a problem with those who disagree with me. Rather, they encourage me to take a second look at my position and consider their points."[232]

---

[226] www.legis.sd.gov.
[227] www.verchioforhouse.com.
[228] In an October 25, 2013 email to the author.
[229] Ibid.
[230] www.legis.sd.gov.
[231] Ibid.
[232] www.verchioforhouse.com.

Lou was aghast that a fellow Italian American didn't want to tout the achievements of his grandfather, and hoped that Verchio would, in fact, take a second look at his own position on the matter. For the record, in 2012, Verchio was the prime sponsor of nine bills, including one designating the American bison as the official mascot of the state of South Dakota and another honoring Cheryl Wait, of Hot Springs, South Dakota, as the 2011 Municipal Finance Officer of the Year.[233]

So much for not wanting to waste taxpayers' money.

* * *

Why leave Del Bianco out of her father's book? Smith Nelson speculated that "there had to be some innocent explanation."[234] And, to her credit, she was able to come up with a theory of her own as to why Rex Allen Smith didn't write about the pride of Port Chester: none of the miners mentioned Luigi in their interviews with him.[235]

It's a plausible theory, especially if one puts any stock in the "self-serving bias" notion alluded to earlier in these pages. Remember, the Keystone miners — who Borglum had indicated objected to Luigi's presence and did not want him in Rapid City — felt unity with one another and distance from Del Bianco.

Luigi's daughter, Gloria, wonders why this was. "Was it because he wasn't on the baseball team?," she asks. "He was a sculptor, his hands were his livelihood, what was he supposed to do? Grab a glove and play ball?"

Foreman George Rumple, whom Gloria recorded at the 50th anniversary celebration in 1991, acknowledged that Luigi "did not make a lot of conversation with a lot of the men."[236]

Further, pointer Matt Reilly, who Caesar and Lou visited with

---

[233] www.legis.sd.gov.
[234] In an August 31, 2013 email to the author.
[235] Ibid.
[236] www.luigimountrushmore.com.

in the same year at his home in Stamford, Connecticut, added that neither the miners nor Luigi socialized with one another. In an audio tape featured on Lou's website, Caesar discusses whether the Keystone miners ever palled around with his father:

> CAESAR: Did he hang around with the men, did he drink with the men, talk with them?
> MATT: No, he wasn't around like that.
> CAESAR: He was a loner, wasn't he?
> MATT: Loner, pertaining to, uh, the work; the men were all whiskey drinkers.
> CAESAR: He what?
> MATT: I said the men were all whiskey drinkers, mostly.
> CAESAR: He was a wine drinker.[237]

"It seems a little odd that neither 'Red' (Anderson) nor any of the other people my dad interviewed would have mentioned Mr. Del Bianco, but I wasn't there for the interviews, so I don't know whether they did or not," she wrote. "I suppose the interview transcripts are somewhere. If so, obviously it would be helpful to read them."[238]

But remember how foreman Rumple was quick to sing Del Bianco's praises? So too was Reilly. Asked by Caesar if his father was the main carver at the monument, Reilly does not equivocate: "Oh yes, Bianco was the main carver."[239]

Questioned whether Luigi was more talented than men such as Anderson or Howard 'Howdy' Peterson, Reilly tells Caesar: "Oh, yes. You can see what ya got up there."[240]

Nevertheless, Smith Nelson was steadfast in her refusal to be-

---

[237] Ibid.
[238] In an August 31, 2013 email to the author.
[239] www.luigimountrushmore.com.
[240] Ibid.

lieve that her father had any bias or dislike against Del Bianco.

"Like everyone, Daddy certainly had flaws as a human being, but deliberately biased research or reporting was emphatically not one of them, so far as I ever saw," she continued.[241] "Daddy didn't operate like that. He'd never leave somebody out of a book because he disliked them," she explained. "His reaction would be to try to figure out what made the guy tick and then, if anything, to write more about them just because this person was an interesting character, somebody different, an anomaly or a variation or whatever.[242]

"I guarantee you — I'd go to court and swear it under oath without a second thought — he knocked himself out to write the most complete, evenhanded, readable book he could," she added.[243]

Like Robert E. Hayes, Smith Nelson also revealed that her father's publisher, Abbeville Press, also cut a chapter from his manuscript due to length.[244]

"Abbeville cut a whole chapter of the Rushmore book before they published it, and now I realize that I don't even know what that missing chapter was about," she wrote. "Of course my dad was upset about losing the chapter, but I gather that kind of thing just happens in publishing. Abbeville didn't want the book to be too long."[245]

Asked about Smith Nelson's comments, Diana Griffin, Abbeville Press' Marketing and Publicity Manager, indicated that her imprint couldn't issue any statement about Luigi's contributions to Mount Rushmore "as Rex Allen Smith is no longer able to offer comments on his work."[246]

But the author wasn't looking for the thoughts of a *dead* man. He was asking whether Abbeville Press thought that publishing a

---

[241] In an August 31, 2013 email to the author.
[242] Ibid.
[243] Ibid.
[244] Ibid.
[245] Ibid.
[246] In an August 28, 2013 email to the author.

book that failed to mention Luigi's role as Mount Rushmore's chief carver somehow discounted its importance.

As this book was going to press, Ms. Griffin still had not responded to *that* question.

Accommodating as ever, Smith Nelson also rued the fact that she couldn't actually find any of her father's Rushmore materials — not the original manuscript, not the transcripts of the interviews, not anything.[247]

"After my dad died in October 2010, I sorted everything on his ranch — which was a herculean task," she wrote.[248] "I boxed up a fraction of what I found and moved it to Lincoln. Among all that I have maybe fifteen or twenty banker's boxes full of my dad's papers. The South Dakota State Historical Society wanted to go through them, which would've been great, but their representative couldn't get out to the ranch until December 15 or so and I had to be out by December 1st."[249]

Some might ask why Smith's failure to include Luigi is so important. After all, *The Carving of Mount Rushmore* is only one book. As has been noted previously, other books have excluded Del Bianco as well. It is the author's opinion, however, that Luigi's exclusion from the Smith book set in motion a ripple effect that helped cause Del Bianco's relative obscurity.

For example, take the Mount Rushmore documentary that first aired as part of the Public Broadcasting System's "The American Experience" series in 2002. Written and produced by Mark Zwonitzer,[250] who won a Writer's Guild of America award in 1997 for an episode of *Frontline* entitled "The Pilgrimage of Jesse Jackson,"[251] the 52-minute Hidden Hill Productions film featured commentary from Robin Borglum Carter as well as Smith, Hayes,

---

[247] In an August 31, 2013 email to the author.
[248] Ibid.
[249] Ibid.
[250] www.pbs.org.
[251] www.imbd.com.

John Sherrill Houser and Clifford, among others.

Narrated by actor Michael Murphy, *Mount Rushmore* clearly used Smith's book as source material. Here is Murphy describing how, after no work occurred for nearly 18 months, due to lack of funding, work at the monument began again in the spring of 1933:

> And the central crew was back: "Hoot" Leach, "Howdy" Peterson and his brother, Merle; Jimmy Champion, "Whiskey" Art Johnson, "Palooka" Payne. They all knew they'd be shut down again for some reason, but they came back just the same.[252]

Not to be outdone, here was Smith himself talking about the miners:

> A lot of these guys were tough, rough brawling kind of guys. They used to say that the Keystone boys' playpens were fenced with barbed wire. And that they only turned the other cheek when they were delivering a left hook....[253]

> One of the great miracles of Rushmore is the miracle of the men, those dedicated guys, the "Red" Andersons, the "Hoot" Leaches, the Peterson boys and so on who came back and came back and came back. [254]

And, lest we forget the man who bills himself as the only known individual still alive who worked at Mount Rushmore, here was part of Clifford's comments:

> Had they not come back, there would be no Mount Rushmore as we know it today because Mr. Borglum, it was impossible for

---

[252] www.pbs.org.
[253] Ibid.
[254] Ibid.

him to train a new crew every year. But these men were dedicated to the mountain. When the mountain would shut down for lack of money or in the wintertime, they'd all have to find another job. But when the spring would come around they'd get the call to come back. They'd quit what they were doing and come back to work at the mountain.[255]

Though the author attempted to contact Zwonitzer, who now works for Apograph Productions in Brooklyn, New York, regarding the source material he utilized, a production manager for the company, Deborah Clancy Porfido, indicated via email in August 2013 that Zwonitzer "is busy writing his own book at the moment. If he has time to respond, I'm sure he will."[256]

Hanna Irfani Appel was the credited researcher on the production. Told by her brother-in-law that a journalist was seeking comments from her, Ms. Appel telephoned the author in September 2013 to say that she "wasn't involved in story or content development at all.

"That was my first job as an archivist," she continued. "I mostly got photographs to use for the documentary. I certainly don't know why Mr. Del Bianco would be left out of it."

"Obviously if Daddy left out Mr. Del Bianco that's a huge omission," Smith Nelson acknowledged. "But, based on my knowledge of my dad, it had to be unintentional."[257]

---

[255] Ibid.
[256] In an August 23, 2013 email to the author.
[257] In an August 31, 2013 email to the author.

CHAPTER 9

"THE SHRINE OF HYPOCRISY"

According to author Adam Pacio, the Sioux Nation consists of seven different tribes, divided into three major groups. The Santee, or "Dakota" group of Sioux which occupied the eastern-most of the Sioux territories contained the Wahpekute, Sisitonwan, Mdewakantonwan, and Wahpetonwan tribes. The Nakota group occupied the central area of Sioux territories and consists of the Yankton and Yanktonai tribes. And the Teton tribe, also called the Lakota, occupied the western Sioux territories.[258]

Although the Sioux were not originally native to the Black Hills, or Paha Sapa as they are called in the Sioux dialects, explains Pacio, the Paha Sapa also became mythically identified as sacred land, with spiritual significance as the place where humanity first emerged from the earth.[259]

Things that are sacred to Native Americans are not always things that are tangible or can be touched. So, while Europeans tended to build places they considered to be sacred, such as churches, statues or memorials, for American Indians sacred places were often not physical things constructed by humans but places and landscapes that were naturally sacred, such as brooks, streams, and rivers.[260]

And mountains.

According to a January 2, 2012 posting that appeared on the webzine Native American Netroots.com, the Black Hills mountain

---

[258] www.rushmore.wingfoot.org.
[259] Ibid.
[260] www.nativeamericannetroots.net.

range of South Dakota was just such a place.[261] So it should come as no surprise that, from the perspective of the Native American, carving busts of United States Presidents on a living, sacred mountain that the Indians believed to be theirs wasn't exactly met with standing ovations by the tribes who lived there. According to the blog, it was the equivalent of painting anti-Christian graffiti outside of a cathedral or anti-Semitic symbols outside a synagogue.[262]

Further, in an online article dated April 14, 2012, the staff of the *Indian Country Today Media Network* observed that "The Lakota Indians and others say that Mount Rushmore isn't just a piece of art they dislike; it's a piece of art they dislike that, to put it in European terms, has been forcibly installed in their own church."[263]

Many Native Americans see those faces on the monument in a far different way than Gutzon Borglum did. Especially since all of them — Washington, Jefferson, Lincoln and Roosevelt — were known for their insensitivity to Indian issues.[264]

In a 2008 column appearing in the *Lakota Country Times*, [265] Tim Giago, an Oglala Lakota Indian who was born, raised and educated on the Pine Ridge Reservation in South Dakota, where the U.S. government unilaterally took land from the American Indians living there in order to establish a gunnery range during World War II, wrote that Teddy Roosevelt used to talk about taking Indian lands by war. "He said, 'It is a primeval warfare and … it is a warfare where no pity is shown to non-combatants'."[266]

He also noted that Lincoln gave the go-ahead to the United States Army to hang 38 Indian warriors in Minnesota, that Jefferson signed off on a deal — the Louisiana Purchase — that took

---

261 Ibid.
262 Ibid.
263 www.indiancountrytodaymedianetwork.com.
264 www.nativeamericannetroots.net.
265 Tim Giago, "Mount Rushmore Seen Through Native Eyes," *Lakota Country Times,* June 12, 2008.
266 Ibid.

millions of acres of land from many Indian tribes without their approval and that Washington ordered the extermination of the Indian people of New England.[267]

The founder and first president of the Native American Journalists Association, Giago added, "You must also remember that Native Americans had a history long before the coming of the white man. Most Indians do not consider the signors of the Declaration of Independence to be their 'Founding Fathers.'"[268]

In a July 2010 column for the *Huffington Post*, Giago pointed out that the Black Hills were never taken legally from the Lakota, Dakota and Nakota Indian tribes, "but were stolen surreptitiously and dishonorably.[269]

"The Fort Laramie Treaty of 1868 put it in writing proclaiming the tribes of the Great Sioux Nation as legal title holders to the Black Hills," he explained.[270]

In his wonderful *Mount Rushmore: An Icon Reconsidered*, author Jesse Larner agrees that, though Mount Rushmore is "in the heart of the Lakota nation ... all its honorees were involved in trying to wipe out the American Indian. The faces therefore are more ironic than iconic, given the manifest destiny philosophy (the concept that held that America was destined to expand from coast to coast) which surrounds the monument."[271]

Larner, who acknowledged to the author in an email that he knew nothing about Luigi Del Bianco, "since the actual construction of the monument was not my main focus, so indeed I am sure that I missed a lot there,"[272] maintains in his book that, though the monument may represent a symbol of pride and glory to "white

---

[267] Ibid.

[268] Ibid.

[269] Tim Giago, "A New Superintendent at Mount Rushmore Memorial," *Huffington Post*, July 27, 2010.

[270] Ibid.

[271] Jesse Larner, *Mount Rushmore; An Icon Reconsidered*, Nation Books, 2002.

[272] In a September 3, 2013 email to the author.

America," in actuality it is nothing but a reminder of how the United States has broken treaties with American Indians and how Native American tribes have gotten hosed over the years.[273]

Most famously, some 350 Lakota men, women and children were slaughtered in 1890 at Wounded Knee, South Dakota in the last major conflict of the American Indian wars. In protest, hundreds of sympathizers occupied Wounded Knee more than eight decades later, in 1973, during a 71-day standoff with federal agents that served to effectively dramatize many historic grievances the Native American population had against the United States government.

In a 2002 interview that aired on C-SPAN's *Booknotes* program, John Taliaferro, the former senior editor at *Newsweek* who authored *Great White Fathers; The Story of the Obsessive Quest to Create Mount Rushmore*, alluded to the breaking of the Laramie Treaty when he told host Brian Lamb that the United States Supreme Court had upheld a Court of Claims decision to award Native Americans $600 million as compensation for the land that was taken from them:

> TALIAFERRO: Well, the Supreme Court, there was a lawsuit filed back in the '20s saying that the Black Hills, the treaty had been violated and the Black Hills had been taken unjustly from the Sioux. It worked all the way through the courts up into the '80s and it went to the Court of Claims and award was given. It was upheld by the Supreme Court, payment for this breach of treaty.
>
> Well, the Lakota Sioux said we don't want this money. We want our Black Hills back. If we take this money it's like wampum. We don't want it. And so it sits in a trust fund in Washington, $600 million now. Six hundred million dollars would help, but this is the strength, this is the passion of the Sioux. This is how badly they want the Black Hills back. They

---

[273] Larner, *Mount Rushmore; An Icon Reconsidered*, Nation Books, 2002.

want Mt. Rushmore back.

LAMB: Who has claim specifically to that $600 million right now?

TALIAFERRO: The Sioux tribe of South Dakota.

LAMB: If they took the money, it would be dispersed among them?

TALIAFERRO: It would be dispersed, yes, and I can't remember what the number would come out to but, you know several thousand dollars per person or obviously maybe it wouldn't be divided person by person. But anyway this is all moot because if there is one thing that the Lakota agree on is we don't want the money. We want what was rightfully ours and they have a good argument.[274]

In the *Encyclopedia of the Great Plains*, David Wishart, of the University of Nebraska, explained that, in *United States v. Sioux Nation of Indians* (1980), the U.S. Supreme Court held that the breaking of the Laramie Treaty by the United States Congress in 1877 constituted a taking of property under the Fifth Amendment, giving rise to an obligation to fairly compensate the Sioux.[275] The Court affirmed a prior decision of the court of claims, which had awarded the Sioux $17.1 million for the taking of the Black Hills, and further held that the tribe was entitled to interest on that amount from 1877.[276]

As of 2009, the monies being held had risen to $900 million. And, while the United States government has recognized that the seizure of land in 1877 was illegal, it is still unwilling to return the Black Hills to the tribes.[277]

According to many American Indian scholars, the monument, which was known to the Sioux as Six Grandfathers, just serves as a

---

[274] www.booknotes.org.

[275] www.plainshumanities.unl.edu.

[276] Ibid.

[277] Chet Brokaw, "Lawsuit Would Let Sioux Take Money for Black Hills," *Native Times*. October 20, 2009.

daily reminder of these painful hurts.[278] Small wonder, therefore, that the late Native American activist Russell C. Means used to refer to Mount Rushmore as "The Shrine of Hypocrisy."[279]

✳ ✳ ✳

In 2004, Gerard Baker, a Mandan-Hidatsa Indian, became the first Native American superintendent of the park. Baker, who grew up on the Fort Berthold Reservation in North Dakota, had previously been superintendent at the Little Bighorn National Battlefield in Montana. When he was offered the position at Mount Rushmore, he called his tribal elders and asked their advice. Unexpectedly, they told him that this would be a good place to start the healing.[280]

Under Baker's leadership, Mount Rushmore opened more avenues of interpretation and moved beyond the single focus on the four Presidents.[281]

In a nine-minute documentary on the monument that was produced and released in 2009 in conjunction with PBS, which was doing a series on the history of the national parks called "Untold Stories," Baker is asked by an interviewer why he has expanded programs at the monument to embrace the vast diversity of cultural traditions and stories that make up our national heritage:

> This is Mount Rushmore! It's America! Everybody's something different here; we're all different. And just maybe that gets us talking again as human beings, as Americans.[282]

---

[278] "A Different View of Mount Rushmore," April 14, 2012, www.indiancountrytodaymedianetwork.com.

[279] Giago, *Lakota Country Times*, June 12, 2008

[280] David Melmer, "Historic Changes for Mount Rushmore," *Indian Country Today*, December 13, 2004.

[281] Giago, "A Man of Great Vision Departs Mount Rushmore," *Huffington Post*, April 19, 2010.

[282] www.pbs.org.

According to an article appearing in a 2008 issue of the *Rapid City Journal*, Baker's efforts to raise cultural awareness included setting up a Heritage Village that featured teepees, a Germans from Russia dance and heritage display and a Sons of Norway crafts and history demonstration. Lakota hoop dancers also performed regularly at the park.[283]

Asked about this in a follow-up email she received from the author, the monument's Director of Interpretative Services, Maureen McGee-Ballinger, explained that the full name of Heritage Village "is the Lakota, Nakota and Dakota Heritage Village. It explores the history of the American Indian tribes who populated the area for thousands of years. The village is normally open June through August. It highlights only local American Indian tribes.[284]

"We have in the past had single day events at which there was a representation of the Germans from Russia, Sons of Norway or a hoop dancer, but not as ongoing exhibits," she added.[285]

At the time of its debut, a spokeswoman for the Park Service's Midwest region, Patty Rooney, said the heritage village "very much" belongs at Rushmore.[286]

"What I'm trying to show here is this place is for everybody," continued Baker, who had a stroke in 2009 and left the agency in 2010. When asked by the *Journal* writer what he would tell people who were turned off by what he and the Park Service were trying to do, namely, expand the number of stories and viewpoints shared at public parks and monuments, Baker simply replied, "I invite them to take their blinders off and look at the full history of this place."[287]

Baker's remarks got the author thinking; if Heritage Village had

---

[283] Barbara Soderlin, "Does Native American Exhibit Belong at Mount Rushmore?", *Rapid City Journal*, August 25, 2008.
[284] In a September 30, 2013 email to the author.
[285] Ibid.
[286] Soderlin, "Does Native American Exhibit Belong at Mount Rushmore?", *Rapid City Journal*, August 25, 2008.
[287] Ibid.

previously featured an occasional Germans from Russia dance and heritage display, as well as periodically showcasing a Sons of Norway crafts and history demonstration, why couldn't Mount Rushmore pay tribute to its Italian-American chief carver?

Michael Reynolds, the NPS' Midwest Regional Director, advised the author in an email that the agency "embraces all of America's stories and people and welcomes your input to improve that relevancy."[288]

Florentine Films — the company which produced the Mount Rushmore segment for PBS — was asked the same question. The documentary's lead producer and writer, Dayton Duncan, told the author in an email that "the sole focus of this brief film was on the fact that an *additional* story is now being told at the Memorial: one that includes the native peoples who considered the place sacred long before the faces were carved."[289]

"Had the focus been on the monumental task of carving those four faces," continued Duncan, "I agree that the story of Luigi Del Bianco would be an important and fascinating component."[290]

Luigi with Native Americans.

---

[288] In a September 29, 2013 email to the author.
[289] In a September 23, 2013 email to the author.
[290] Ibid.

CHAPTER 10

"THIS COUNTRY OWES HIM THE LOVE"

Andre DiMino is the executive director of UNICO National. A past National President of the organization, which was founded in 1922 and is the largest Italian-American service and charitable group in the country, he understandably has some strong feelings regarding Luigi's work at the monument.

"The amazing legacy of Luigi Del Bianco is a source of pride, not only for Americans of Italian heritage, but for every American," says DiMino.[291] "His involvement in the realization of one of the most iconic symbols of America is a testament to his determination, artistry, and craftsmanship. Thanks to Luigi Del Bianco the massive visages of Mount Rushmore stand as an everlasting monument to the indelible imprint Italian immigrants have had on our great country."[292]

Glenn Guerriero, who co-owns Brooklyn Attitude Hair and Body with his wife, Mary Ann, can attest to that immigrant imprint. A second-generation Italian American whose great-grandparents hailed from Calabria, Italy, Guerriero's great-grandfather, Domenico Rocco Quattrone, was a barber as well.

"I never met my great-grandfather but I know he would be proud of me for my achievements in the beauty profession and carrying on his tradition," says Guerriero.[293] The couple's Saratoga Springs, New York business has consistently been voted among the top one hundred hair salons in the country for the past six years by *BE! Beauty Entertainment Magazine*.

---

[291] In a October 25, 2013 email to the author.
[292] Ibid.
[293] In a November 17, 2013 email to the author.

"In my eyes my great-grandfather is getting his due credit, unlike Luigi," continues Guerriero.[294] "Luigi Del Bianco carved his way into American history, and that's why I will always be grateful to people like him. He was a trailblazer, a true pioneer. Immigrants like my great-grandfather and Luigi made it easier for individuals such as myself to succeed in this country."[295]

Members of Congress have also picked up on the fact that the work Luigi did at the monument is a testament to the immigrant contribution to the history of the United States.

United States Representative Pat Tiberi, who represents Ohio's 12th Congressional District in the House of Representatives, chairs the Italian-American Congressional Delegation. Asked what he thought about Lou's efforts to gain some kind of recognition for Luigi, Representative Tiberi was very supportive.

"Luigi Del Bianco's story is an inspiration to many," Representative Tiberi said through his spokesperson.[296] "From growing up in Italy, to raising a family in the United States, his immigration story reverberates through generations of Americans. Luigi left his mark on some of the most recognizable monuments in our nation, most notably bringing Lincoln's eyes to life on the faces at Mt. Rushmore."[297]

"Luigi's dedication and skill are seen every day by Americans and visitors alike and should be formally recognized and his contributions remembered," he added.[298]

Five days after the occasion of the monument's 50th anniversary, Tiberi's colleague, United States Representative Nita M. Lowey, stood up on the floor of the House of Representatives and echoed similar sentiments, warmly praising Luigi as the man who helped

---

[294] Ibid.
[295] Ibid.
[296] In a September 25, 2013 email to the author.
[297] Ibid.
[298] Ibid.

carve Mount Rushmore.[299]

The Ranking Member on the House Committee on Appropriations, Lowey made special mention of the fact that Luigi, who became an American citizen on January 13, 1928, always "cherished" that status.[300]

"Luigi Del Bianco always exemplified the best of America," said Lowey, who still represents Port Chester in the House.[301] "Through his art and his upstanding character, Luigi Del Bianco, who came to this country as an immigrant, became an integral part of his community and his Nation."[302]

"An artist and craftsman, educated in stonecutting and carving in Austria, he understood that hard work and dedication is the only sure route to success," added Lowey.[303] "His dedication to both his native and adopted countries and his appreciation of his rich heritage was evident when he returned to Italy to defend it against its Austro-Hungarian invaders in World War I, fighting in the Italian Army alongside American and Allied troops.[304]

"In the finest American tradition, he helped in shaping its most famous monument," she continued. "His life and his work reminds us of the greatness of the American ideal which we celebrate on Independence Day."[305]

"Luigi Del Bianco was truly a man who made a great impression on his neighbors, an immigrant who exemplified the great American values of hard work and dedication to this country, and a fine artist who made an indelible contribution to the United States," concluded Lowey.[306] "As we celebrate our Nation's 215th

---

[299] Congressional Record, 102nd Congress, July 9, 1991.
[300] Ibid.
[301] Ibid.
[302] Ibid.
[303] Ibid.
[304] Ibid.
[305] Ibid.
[306] Ibid.

birthday, and the 50th anniversary of his great work, I am sure my colleagues will join me in remembering and honoring Luigi Del Bianco, who, through the work of his own hands, has left much for this Nation of ours. His works have been an inspiration to many."[307]

Fast forward 22 years, to March 2013 and, as he grew more and more upset over the Park Service's refusal to recognize his grandfather's work, Lou contacted Representative Lowey's White Plains office.

A decade earlier, he had also reached out to Lowey's office for assistance. At that time, he spoke with her then-aide, George Latimer, who now represents Port Chester in the New York State Senate. This time, the Congresswoman's office drafted correspondence that was sent to Elaine Hackett, the Congressional liaison to the Park Service. In it, Lowey reminds Hackett that Luigi's work on one of America's iconic memorials "is a testament to the immigrant contribution to the history of this country."[308]

In the short term, Representative Lowey's letter had the desired effect. Lou was put in touch with Reynolds, the Midwestern Director for the agency who was initially supportive of what he was attempting to do, namely, get the agency to recognize Luigi in a meaningful way.

Reynolds, who Lou claims now refuses to return his calls, replied promptly to Lowey's letter the very next month, in May 2013.

"As we have discussed with Mr. Del Bianco, the NPS celebrates all who have worked on the sculpture," wrote Reynolds.[309] But then Reynolds pointed out to Lowey that the monument wasn't about one man, rather, it was a communal effort — the very same argument that sculptors John Lopez and John Sherrill Houser had also made to the author in two separate emails:

---

[307] Ibid.
[308] April 10, 2013 letter to Elaine Hackett.
[309] May 7. 2013 letter from Michael Reynolds to Representative Lowey.

Although Hugo Villa, William S. Tallman and Lincoln Borglum all supervised the project during periods when Gutzon Borglum was absent, and Lincoln Borglum became the Superintendent of the site and completed the carving after his father's death, none of these other workers or other men are called out for special recognition. The expertise of many contributed to the success of the sculpture. If not for the dynamite experts, the carvers would not have had good rock exposed with which to work. If not for the expert blacksmiths fabricating new tools, maintaining drill bits and keeping equipment in working order, the drillers would not have been able to make the holes for the blasters. All of the workers were essential to achieving the ultimate goals. We do not have the space, budget or staff to develop special exhibits for each of these individuals. All of these men are celebrated in the same way on the worker's wall and in the museum. We recognize and interpret one Master Carver — the artist himself — Gutzon Borglum.[310]

We appreciate Mr. Del Bianco's dedication to his grandfather and hope that he will recognize the value of his grandfather working as part of a team that created an unprecedented masterpiece.[311]

Like the hammer hitting the nail, Reynolds's remarks do seemingly strike right to the heart of the matter. However, while there is no greater advocate of the "There is no I in TEAM" philosophy than the author, there still seems to be something flawed in grouping men like Elwood Iverson, who cut lodgepole pine to make scaffolding, or Edwald Hayes, who ran a lift elevator up to the top of the mountain, together with the likes of Luigi. Or even Villa and Tallman, for that matter.

---

[310] Ibid.
[311] Ibid.

By lumping all the workers together, irrespective of their roles, the Park Service seems to be suggesting that jobs at the monument were interchangeable. That a man like Clifford could do Luigi's work, and vice versa. But on the face of it, that's a ridiculous supposition. For instance, would you expect a taxi cab driver to be good at teaching? The author personally knows many substitute teachers who have supplemented their incomes by moonlighting behind the wheel as taxi cab drivers. But more than likely, the opposite would probably not be true. How many regular taxi cab drivers have passed the certification exams and satisfied the licensure requirements necessary to teach at a school?

Similarly, one could imagine Villa, Tallman or Luigi being able to run an elevator lift, or cut lodgepole pine. But it was probably unlikely that either Iverson or Hayes could do the work that Luigi, Villa or Tallman did.

To be sure, Reynolds is not entirely unsympathetic when it comes to appreciating Lou's position. "It is understandable that the Del Bianco family wishes to herald the involvement of its ancestor in carving the Memorial Structure," he wrote to the author, in a letter sent via email on October 23rd. But by the same token, both he and the agency refuse to budge from their position.[312]

"Let me assure you that NPS interpretation of American history is not static, but ever evolving," added Reynolds, referring to the author's observations about the seemingly selective kind of multiculturalism practiced by the agency.[313] He explained that, when funding for the project becomes available, an official baseline document called the Historic Resource Study would help complete historical documentation of the park's story and sources by surveying and synthesizing all primary and secondary source material pertinent to the memorial.[314]

---

[312] In a September 26, 2013 letter to the author.
[313] Ibid.
[314] Ibid.

"This will include all contributors to the Memorial's development, including the important role played by the late Mr. Del Bianco," concluded Reynolds.[315]

In the interim, Lou says he received a phone call in early October 2013 from no less than McGee-Ballinger herself, offering him the opportunity to "make a recording about Luigi for the Mount Rushmore website as part of their oral history link. This is being made available to the descendants of the 'workers' to talk about their time on the mountain."

Afterwards, he equated the offer to throwing him a bone.

Like Lou, Latimer is unimpressed. "Dangling hundreds of feet in the air, defying injury or death, Luigi Del Bianco showed the love for his adopted country by lovingly sculpting the faces of its greatest heroes," said Latimer, a member of the Italian American State Legislators Conference.[316] A bipartisan organization of New York State Assembly and Senate members who are actively involved in promoting and celebrating the state's Italian-American community, the Conference mission is to work hard to elevate and highlight Italian-American contributions to the State of New York and beyond, in all aspects of society, including literature, the arts, architecture and politics. The conference also tries to dispel negative stereotypes of Italian Americans.

"This country owes Luigi Del Bianco the love — the recognition — of his accomplishment," added Latimer.[317]

South Dakota's Small Business Person of the Year in 2011, Leigh Kamstra, the owner and head chef at Roma's Restaurante, in Spearfish, South Dakota, agrees with Latimer. Though conceding that she had never heard of Luigi Del Bianco, Kamstra, who received a United States Small Business Administration 504 loan of

---

[315] Ibid.
[316] In a October 7, 2013 email to the author.
[317] Ibid.

almost $600,000 to expand her facilities four years ago,[318] essentially maintained that attention had to be paid.

"If he was a key player in Mount Rushmore," she told the author via a Facebook message, "then recognition should be given where it's due."[319]

Luigi Del Bianco with Lincoln Borglum.

---

[318] www.sba.gov.
[319] In an October 7, 2013 message to the author.

EPILOGUE

Due to a dispute over the Affordable Care Act, and the resulting failure of Congress to approve funding for the United States government's operations, effective October 1, 2013, many national parks were forced to close due to the federal shutdown.

Mount Rushmore was among them.

The monument's closure was bad enough. As a columnist in *The Sioux Falls Argus Leader* observed, "Blocking access to trails and programs at South Dakota's most popular attraction was one thing, but state officials didn't expect Congress' budget stalemate to shut down a view of Mount Rushmore."[320]

For whatever the reason, the Park Service helped add fuel to the fire by placing cones along highway viewing areas outside of Mount Rushmore, barring individuals from pulling over in their cars and taking pictures of the famed monument.[321]

Do people, in general, and government agencies, in particular, make bad choices? Of course they do. No less than one of the presidents the monument pays tribute to — Thomas Jefferson — is widely credited with declaring that, "My reading of history convinces me that most bad government results from too much government."

So onerous was this decision by the agency that, in the midst of the impasse caused by the government shutdown, state politicians on both sides of the aisle were in agreement that the Park Service had overstepped its bounds and was left with egg on its face.

"It disgusts me that taxpayer resources were used on this act of

---

[320] Jonathan Ellis, "Rushmore Blockage Stirs Anger in South Dakota," *The Sioux Falls Argus Leader,* October 5, 2013.
[321] Ibid.

stupidity," said Kristi Noem, a Republican who is the state's lone member of the House of Representatives. "This is federal government arrogance at its worst."[322]

"They won't even let you pull off on the side of the road," said State Tourism Secretary Jim Hagen said. "I just don't know what they're trying to accomplish."[323]

And Perry Plumart, a spokesman for Democratic Senator Tim Johnson, told the paper that closing Mount Rushmore hurt "visitors, businesses and furloughed park rangers."[324]

Thanks to donations from the private sector, on Monday, October 14, 2013, the monument reopened, courtesy of the $15,200 the Mount Rushmore Society had agreed to pony up in a deal brokered between South Dakota Governor Dennis Daugaard and the Park Service.[325]

All told, 16 other contributors — including the Cliffords — volunteered to contribute the monies just to keep Mount Rushmore open to the public.[326]

The announcement from the Governor's office came two days before a deal was hammered out in both the United States House of Representatives and the United States Senate that ended the shutdown.

Ironically enough, the second Monday of the month turned out to be Columbus Day — the holiday that South Dakota chooses not to acknowledge.

For the author, the government shutdown only served to crystallize the entire brouhaha over Luigi's contributions to the monument. Because of some conscious choice the Park Service made years ago, Luigi Del Bianco has not been acknowledged as the chief carver at Mount Rushmore.

---

[322] Ibid.
[323] Ibid.
[324] Ibid.
[325] www.news.sd.gov.
[326] Ibid.

While bias, bigotry and prejudice have no doubt exacerbated the situation, it's the Park Service's consistent failure to modify its own position that flies in the face of the very concept of multiculturalism the agency claims to be a proponent of.

Surely, the brass at both the United States Department of the Interior and the Park Service understand that change is a natural by-product of growth. If it wasn't, Americans would never have a reason to discuss the Bill of Rights — the first ten amendments to the United States Constitution that were passed in 1791.

And, since there have been 17 additional amendments to that great document over the ensuing 223 years of this country's history — the 27th amendment was passed in 1992 — it's not a stretch to suggest that there might be a few more in our nation's future.

Similarly, thanks to Gerard Baker, if the Park Service could add a Heritage Village that featured teepees, a Germans from Russia dance and heritage display, and a Sons of Norway crafts and history demonstration, it seems the agency could also find room to tout the accomplishments of its Italian-American chief carver from 1933 through 1940.

In the author's way of thinking, that would be a good choice.

Coincidentally, the title track from one of Lou's critically acclaimed CDs is called *Make A Good Choice*. It is also the name of one of the 45-minute programs he performs during school assemblies.

The program, which is tailored for both kindergarten through second grades, as well as grades three through six, sees Lou take his audience on a journey back through his childhood. In it, he shares the daily joys, dreams and blunders that children can relate to, laugh at and understand.

Make A Good Choice, which weaves such character education themes as respect, honesty, kindness, tolerance, cooperation and responsibility into its message, asks children what kinds of choices they would make if they were in Lou's shoes and how those choices reflect on their own lives.

With regards to his efforts vis-à-vis his late grandfather, Lou clearly has made the choice to honor his memory. According to him, that's how *In the Shadow of the Mountain* was born.

"It's a show about many things," explains Lou. "It's a story about history. Children leave my show learning that sometimes history isn't always 'in stone'".

"I think the show gives kids a whole new perspective on how we should read all different sides of history to have a more well-rounded sense of it," he continues. "It is also a show about heritage. I always tell school children to go and talk to their parents and grandparents and find out their life stories. It's a wonderful way to connect with our ancestors and keep the family history alive for future generations. We should never forget where we come from, and hearing a touching story from a grandparent can help us remember.

"Finally, it's a show about America," adds Lou. "It's a show about an immigrant who came to America to live the American dream."

As the grandson of Italian immigrants, Kenneth Orrock, the elected prosecutor at the Office of the Bennett County State's Attorney, in Bennett County, South Dakota, knows exactly where Lou is coming from. "The contributions of Italian immigrants to the western United States have been greatly overlooked by history," he told the author in an email.[327]

"From the development of the California wine industry to the carving of America's Shrine of Democracy at Mount Rushmore, Italian Americans helped settle and tame the west," continued Orrock. "Not only through their energies and enterprise, but by bringing to this new country the old world skills and artistry that have left long lasting monuments to our nation and its unique culture."[328]

---

[327] In an October 17, 2013 email to the author.
[328] Ibid.

The state's capitol, in Pierre, South Dakota, is proof positive of that. According to the South Dakota Bureau of Administration, the permanent capitol was built between 1905 and 1910; the building, which takes up 114,000 square feet, is 161 feet tall, 190 feet wide and 292 feet long.[329]

Built in the Classic Revival style, it has handcrafted woodwork, brass, and stonework. The ornate rotunda dome features marble balustrades and columns, and stained-glass skylights.[330]

Italian workers reportedly laid the capitol's terrazzo tile floor, according to the South Dakota Historical Society Foundation. In a February 2013 newsletter article entitled "Legends of the Capitol," the Foundation noted that, though almost all the marble tiles in the Capitol's floors are yellow, rust, white, black, tan and green, 66 of them are said to be blue.[331]

Each of the 66 Italian workers who laid the floor during the Capitol's 1905-1910 construction was given a blue stone to place anywhere in the Capitol as a "signature stone." To date, 57 of the special tiles have supposedly been found.[332]

Informed of this, Lou says he would love it if a special stone were placed somewhere on the grounds of Mount Rushmore in recognition of Luigi's work.

But whatever else he is or isn't, Lou Del Bianco is a pragmatist. And he knows that the first step on the way to achieving his goals is to raise awareness.

He got an unlikely, and unexpected assist, from the former president of the Mount Rushmore Society.

Though current Society President Knight and Executive Director Saathoff consistently failed to return the author's repeated emails requesting statements from them both, the Immediate Past Presi-

---

[329] www.state.sd.us
[330] www.nps.gov.
[331] www.sdhsf.org.
[332] Ibid.

dent of the group, Ruth Samuelsen, was more than happy to volunteer to write about Luigi's important work at the monument.

"As you may or may not know," she wrote in mid-September 2013, "the Society is a sponsor of the annual Naturalization Ceremony at the mountain every summer. At this summer event, approximately 100 people are sworn in by the United States District Court. It is a lovely and truly memorable ceremony.[333]

"I have had the privilege of speaking at this event for three summers, in 2009, 2010, and in 2011," continued Samuelsen. "At the 2009 ceremony I featured and honored Mr. Del Bianco as a fellow immigrant who was the chief carver of the mountain, and challenged the new citizens to rise to his level of immortality."[334]

"I think it was truly inspirational to the new citizens that an immigrant worker rose to such heights, literally and figuratively," concluded Samuelsen.[335]

It's a start, the author said to himself. And on the road to truth, that counts for a lot.

---

[333] In a September 15, 2013 email to the author.
[334] Ibid.
[335] Ibid.

INDEX

ABOUT THE AUTHOR

DOUGLAS J. GLADSTONE is a journalist by training, whose published articles have appeared in *The Chicago Sun Times*, *The Burlington Free Press* and *History Magazine*, among others.

His critically acclaimed 2010 book, *A Bitter Cup of Coffee; How MLB & The Players Association Threw 874 Retirees A Curve*, is widely credited with helping retired Major League Baseball (MLB) players who were without pensions receive financial compensation from MLB. *Carving A Niche for Himself* is his second book.

VIA FOLIOS

A refereed book series dedicated to the culture of Italians and Italian Americans.

MARIA TERRONE. *Eye to Eye.* Vol 94 Poetry. $14

CONSTANCE SANCETTA. *Here in Cerchio* Vol 93 Local History. $15

MARIA MAZZIOTTI GILLAN. *Ancestors' Song* Vol 92 Poetry. $14

DARRELL FUSARO. *What if Godzilla Just Wanted a Hug?* Vol ? Essays. $TBA

MICHAEL PARENTI. *Waiting for Yesterday: Pages from a Street Kid's Life.* Vol 90 Memoir. $15

ANNIE LANZILOTTO, *Schistsong*, Vol. 89. Poetry, $15

EMANUEL DI PASQUALE, *Love Lines*, Vol. 88. Poetry, $10

CAROSONE & LOGIUDICE. *Our Naked Lives.* Vol 87 Essays. $15

JAMES PERICONI. *Strangers in a Strange Land: A Survey of Italian-Language American Books.* Vol. 86. Book History. $24

DANIELA GIOSEFFI, *Escaping La Vita Della Cucina*, Vol. 85. Essays & Creative Writing. $22

MARIA FAMÀ, *Mystics in the Family*, Vol. 84. Poetry, $10

ROSSANA DEL ZIO, *From Bread and Tomatoes to Zuppa di Pesce "Ciambotto"*, Vol. 83. $15

LORENZO DELBOCA, *Polentoni*, Vol. 82. Italian Studies, $15

SAMUEL GHELLI, *A Reference Grammar*, Vol. 81. Italian Language. $36

ROSS TALARICO, *Sled Run*, Vol. 80. Fiction. $15

FRED MISURELLA, *Only Sons*, Vol. 79. Fiction. $14

FRANK LENTRICCHIA, *The Portable Lentricchia*, Vol. 78. Fiction. $16

RICHARD VETERE, *The Other Colors in a Snow Storm*, Vol. 77. Poetry. $10

GARIBALDI LAPOLLA, *Fire in the Flesh*, Vol. 76 Fiction & Criticism. $25

GEORGE GUIDA, *The Pope Stories*, Vol. 75 Prose. $15

ROBERT VISCUSI, *Ellis Island*, Vol. 74. Poetry. $28

ELENA GIANINI BELOTTI, *The Bitter Taste of Strangers Bread*, Vol. 73, Fiction, $24

PINO APRILE, *Terroni*, Vol. 72, Italian Studies, $20

EMANUEL DI PASQUALE, *Harvest*, Vol. 71, Poetry, $10

ROBERT ZWEIG, *Return to Naples*, Vol. 70, Memoir, $16

AIROS & CAPPELLI, *Guido*, Vol. 69, Italian/American Studies, $12

FRED GARDAPHÉ, *Moustache Pete is Dead! Long Live Moustache Pete!*, Vol. 67, Literature/Oral History, $12

PAOLO RUFFILLI, *Dark Room/Camera oscura*, Vol. 66, Poetry, $11

HELEN BAROLINI, *Crossing the Alps*, Vol. 65, Fiction, $14

COSMO FERRARA, *Profiles of Italian Americans*, Vol. 64, Italian Americana, $16

GIL FAGIANI, *Chianti in Connecticut*, Vol. 63, Poetry, $10

BASSETTI & D'ACQUINO, *Italic Lessons*, Vol. 62, Italian/American Studies, $10

CAVALIERI & PASCARELLI, Eds., *The Poet's Cookbook*, Vol. 61, Poetry/Recipes, $12

EMANUEL DI PASQUALE, *Siciliana*, Vol. 60, Poetry, $8

NATALIA COSTA, Ed., *Bufalini*, Vol. 59, Poetry. $18.

RICHARD VETERE, *Baroque*, Vol. 58, Fiction. $18.

LEWIS TURCO, *La Famiglia/The Family*, Vol. 57, Memoir, $15

NICK JAMES MILETI, *The Unscrupulous*, Vol. 56, Humanities, $20

BASSETTI, ACCOLLA, D'AQUINO, *Italici: An Encounter with Piero Bassetti*, Vol. 55, Italian Studies, $8

GIOSE RIMANELLI, *The Three-legged One*, Vol. 54, Fiction, $15

CHARLES KLOPP, *Bele Antiche Stòrie*, Vol. 53, Criticism, $25

Bordighera Press is an imprint of Bordighera, Incorporated, an independently owned not-for-profit scholarly organization that has no legal affiliation with the University of Central Florida or with The John D. Calandra Italian American Institute, Queens College/CUNY.

JOSEPH RICAPITO, *Second Wave*, Vol. 52, Poetry, $12
GARY MORMINO, *Italians in Florida*, Vol. 51, History, $15
GIANFRANCO ANGELUCCI, *Federico F.*, Vol. 50, Fiction, $15
ANTHONY VALERIO, *The Little Sailor*, Vol. 49, Memoir, $9
ROSS TALARICO, *The Reptilian Interludes*, Vol. 48, Poetry, $15
RACHEL GUIDO DE VRIES, *Teeny Tiny Tino's Fishing Story*, Vol. 47, Children's Literature, $6
EMANUEL DI PASQUALE, *Writing Anew*, Vol. 46, Poetry, $15
MARIA FAMÀ, *Looking For Cover*, Vol. 45, Poetry, $12
ANTHONY VALERIO, *Toni Cade Bambara's One Sicilian Night*, Vol. 44, Poetry, $10
EMANUEL CARNEVALI, Dennis Barone, Ed., *Furnished Rooms*, Vol. 43, Poetry, $14
BRENT ADKINS, et al., Ed., *Shifting Borders, Negotiating Places*, Vol. 42, Proceedings, $18
GEORGE GUIDA, *Low Italian*, Vol. 41, Poetry, $11
GARDAPHÈ, GIORDANO, TAMBURRI, *Introducing Italian Americana*, Vol. 40, Italian/American
     Studies, $10
DANIELA GIOSEFFI, *Blood Autumn/Autunno di sangue*, Vol. 39, Poetry, $15/$25
FRED MISURELLA, *Lies to Live by*, Vol. 38, Stories, $15
STEVEN BELLUSCIO, *Constructing a Bibliography*, Vol. 37, Italian Americana, $15
ANTHONY JULIAN TAMBURRI, Ed., *Italian Cultural Studies 2002*, Vol. 36, Essays, $18
BEA TUSIANI, *con amore*, Vol. 35, Memoir, $19
FLAVIA BRIZIO-SKOV, Ed., *Reconstructing Societies in the Aftermath of War*, Vol. 34, History, $30
TAMBURRI, et al., Eds., *Italian Cultural Studies 2001*, Vol. 33, Essays, $18
ELIZABETH G. MESSINA, Ed., *In Our Own Voices*, Vol. 32, Italian/American Studies, $25
STANISLAO G. PUGLIESE, *Desperate Inscriptions*, Vol. 31, History, $12
HOSTERT & TAMBURRI, Eds., *Screening Ethnicity*, Vol. 30, Italian/American Culture, $25
G. PARATI & B. LAWTON, Eds., *Italian Cultural Studies*, Vol. 29, Essays, $18
HELEN BAROLINI, *More Italian Hours*, Vol. 28, Fiction, $16
FRANCO NASI, Ed., *Intorno alla Via Emilia*, Vol. 27, Culture, $16
ARTHUR L. CLEMENTS, *The Book of Madness & Love*, Vol. 26, Poetry, $10
JOHN CASEY, et al., *Imagining Humanity*, Vol. 25, Interdisciplinary Studies, $18
ROBERT LIMA, *Sardinia/Sardegna*, Vol. 24, Poetry, $10
DANIELA GIOSEFFI, *Going On*, Vol. 23, Poetry, $10
ROSS TALARICO, *The Journey Home*, Vol. 22, Poetry, $12
EMANUEL DI PASQUALE, *The Silver Lake Love Poems*, Vol. 21, Poetry, $7
JOSEPH TUSIANI, *Ethnicity*, Vol. 20, Poetry, $12
JENNIFER LAGIER, *Second Class Citizen*, Vol. 19, Poetry, $8
FELIX STEFANILE, *The Country of Absence*, Vol. 18, Poetry, $9
PHILIP CANNISTRARO, *Blackshirts*, Vol. 17, History, $12
LUIGI RUSTICHELLI, Ed., *Seminario sul racconto*, Vol. 16, Narrative, $10
LEWIS TURCO, *Shaking the Family Tree*, Vol. 15, Memoirs, $9
LUIGI RUSTICHELLI, Ed., *Seminario sulla drammaturgia*, Vol. 14, Theater/Essays, $10
FRED GARDAPHÈ, *Moustache Pete is Dead! Long Live Moustache Pete!*, Vol. 13, Oral Literature,
     $10
JONE GAILLARD CORSI, *Il libretto d'autore*, 1860–1930, Vol. 12, Criticism, $17
HELEN BAROLINI, *Chiaroscuro: Essays of Identity*, Vol. 11, Essays, $15
PICARAZZI & FEINSTEIN, Eds., *An African Harlequin in Milan*, Vol. 10, Theater/Essays, $15
JOSEPH RICAPITO, *Florentine Streets & Other Poems*, Vol. 9, Poetry, $9
FRED MISURELLA, *Short Time*, Vol. 8, Novella, $7
NED CONDINI, *Quartettsatz*, Vol. 7, Poetry, $7
ANTHONY JULIAN TAMBURRI, Ed., *Fuori: Essays by Italian/American Lesbians and Gays*, Vol. 6,
     Essays, $10

ANTONIO GRAMSCI, P. Verdicchio, Trans. & Intro. , *The Southern Question*, Vol. 5, Social Criticism, $5

DANIELA GIOSEFFI, *Word Wounds & Water Flowers*, Vol. 4, Poetry, $8

WILEY FEINSTEIN, *Humility's Deceit: Calvino Reading Ariosto Reading Calvino*, Vol. 3, Criticism, $10

PAOLO A. GIORDANO, Ed., *Joseph Tusiani: Poet, Translator, Humanist*, Vol. 2, Criticism, $25

ROBERT VISCUSI, *Oration Upon the Most Recent Death of Christopher Columbus*, Vol. 1, Poetry, $3

CPSIA information can be obtained at www.ICGtesting.com
Printed in the USA
BVOW11s1234250714

360429BV00008B/106/P